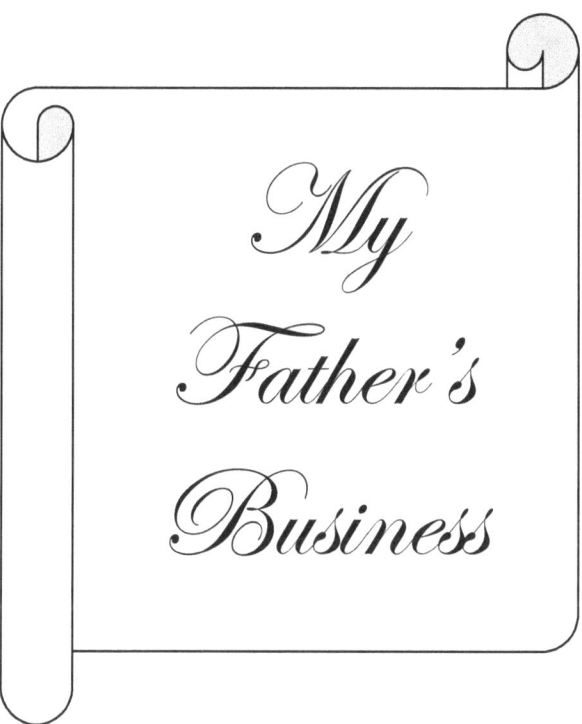

Written by Darold Edwards

Copyright © 2008 Darold F. Edwards
Editing Assistance by MyKeyWeb.com

My Father's Business

Table of Contents:

i.	Introduction	5
ii.	Acknowledgments	15
iii.	Preface	19
I.	My Father's Business	25
II.	Jesus Our Hope	37
III.	Love	59
IV.	Whose Children Are They?	69
V.	Bible Only	89
VI.	One Gospel, Two Messages	111
VII.	Peace	123
VIII.	People	139
IX.	Life or Existence	149
X.	The Exceptions	159
XI.	Greatness	173
XII.	What Good Have We Done	179
XIII.	The Garbage Collector	189
XIV.	The Prosperous Soul	197

NOTES

i.   A General Introduction to
The Works of

Darold Edwards

I would like to begin this introduction of myself and my writings with a greeting to all who are gracious enough to take the time to read these writings and join me in this journey of Bible exploration and study. This greeting is found in [2 Peter 1: 2], "Grace and peace be multiplied to you through the knowledge of God, and of Jesus our Lord". In [Galatians 2: 6] Paul writes of people "who added nothing to me". It is my desire and prayer that these writings will add much to you in your Bible explorations and enrichment of life.

Let me introduce myself to you. It is very likely you have never heard of me but that is alright, as I have never heard of the vast majority of you, but, I know you are out there somewhere in our big wide world that seems to be getting smaller with a disturbing amount of consistency. At the present time I am 75 years old, and like most of everything else in this world, my age is subject to constant change. My wife of 52, going on 53years of marriage, Patricia, is a very wonderful person who has had the grace to put up with me these many years gone by and has been a constant source of help, strength, and encouragement to me; with a little challenge thrown in from time to time to help keep life interesting. But having no complaints, I am looking forward to a continuation of our life together, at least for some time to come. We have our home in Albany, Oregon, raised 3 children there and have grandchildren and great grandchildren.

After a privileged time as a child and young person under the care and guidance of some very wonderful loving parents, I proceeded on to adulthood with an average course of life doing some things I should and some that I shouldn't. My specific vocation, after various jobs, was about 42 years as an electrician which was enjoyed very much. In the latter portion of this time I was able and blessed to assist in many church construction jobs as an electrician. There came a time, however, that my body convinced me it was time to seek other easier things to do. After that career ran its course and was fading into the sunset, I was led into an interest in writing, which is where I am today and will probably be for the remainder of my time on this earth. I am enjoying it with much satisfaction, and what you see here is among the beginnings of it. I hope you will blessed by it.

My main interest and priority is and has been in pursuit of Biblical study and knowledge for several years. As I get an ever increasing "vision of the value" of such study and exploration, the interest and priority increases accordingly. This Biblical knowledge with its provision of life and life more abundantly through Jesus Christ our Lord, indeed has become my life with its great and perfect peace with joy unspeakable and full of glory. What a blessed state of being to enjoy an unending hope and blessed assurance of a future that extends from today on to and including eternity.

Not being very impressed with humanity in its general condition and what it has done to this world God has provided for it, much of my writings will be addressing this issue and whose responsible for such a degraded condition as this world is in, including our "Land of the Free and the Home of the Brave". You may not agree with me in some of my views and interpretations, but it is only important that you be in agreement with Jesus. Some of the positions I take on traditional Bible interpretations will be somewhat controversial, maybe even viewed as heretical by some, but will certainly provide reason for some new exploration of thinking and thought. God tells us in [Isaiah 55: 8-9], "My thoughts are not your thoughts, neither are my ways your ways, saith the Lord. For as the heavens are higher than the earth, so are my ways higher than your ways, and my thoughts than your thoughts".

So as we re-explore some of these old traditional truths and absolutes of God's Word that have brought life, strength, stability, and comfort to all who embrace them, lets keep our minds open to other additional concepts, original ideas, thoughts and ways that are a part of the expanse between where we are today and where God is calling us to be. I do not believe, that in the fullness of God's greatness, man has reached the end of all God has for us to think about either in the knowledge we are to gain or in the development of our mental capabilities. Much education and knowledge lay before us yet to be attained to. Once again, it is not important that you agree with me, but don't get caught in disagreement with God and his Word, that is a fatal mistake that is much to prevalent in our world today.

My writings are not meant to be entertaining, though a bit of mirth from time to time is acceptable. Yet encouragement and inspiration for meditation and diligent, committed study for spiritual growth and development resulting in intimate fellowship and relationship with God and our Saviour and Lord Jesus Christ is, and remains, the priority. I will be using some words that may offend some but are meant only to describe some very apparent conditions that are alive, yet actually more sick than well, thriving and somewhat destructive, in humanity. God is much more of a gentleman than I am and limits his language to words such as fool, fools, and foolishness. I get a little rougher in my references to mankind and use words such as stupid, idiotic, ignorance etc.

Please understand I have nothing against people, only against the conditions listed above, stupidity, idiocy, and ignorance, etc, that humanity has such an overwhelming desire to wallow and remain in to the degradation of themselves, their societies, and nations, when God, in his love, has given us the remedy for deliverance from such nonsense. To refuse, or neglect, to avail oneself of what God has made available for deliverance from sin and its results, does in itself, put an individuals and a societies intelligence in very serious question.

You are certainly welcome to disagree with me and raise an argument in protest if you wish, however, just a little insight and understanding of the condition our nation is in, and how it arrived at this state of demise from the abominations of sin and iniquity of its inhabitants should settle the argument and any questions about it once and for all.

I do hope to wake many minds that have gone to sleep to the challenge of some new in-depth thought that will project them into new ways of life and living where "the heart is diligently kept, clean, and guarded" [Proverbs 4:23], the mind and spirit are renewed, [Romans 12: 2; Psalms 51:10], and the soul prospers" [3 John: 2]. If we continue to think the way we've always thought, we'll continue to get what we've always got. Much of our traditional thinking has lulled us to sleep, resulting in the unchallenged abdicating of our dominion authority to the enemy and his ever willing assistants. The way humanity is digressing, we cannot afford to continue along that road of demented mentality, either as individuals or as a nation.

It is my intention that other books will be written as the inspiration to do so presents itself. Several others are already in the works, all dealing with Biblical truths as they relate to the problems and dilemmas of our present day and time; all based on man's disobedience and rebellion against God, His truth and absolutes. This has been the story down through the ages and has only intensified as the population of man has increased, [Hosea 4: 7], "As they were increased, so they sinned against me: therefore I will change their glory into shame". It is this increase in intensity of disobedience, rebellion, sin, iniquity, etc, etc, call it what you will, that has proven so disastrous to mankind, that prompts referral to the conditions of stupidity, idiocy, and ignorance with which man has so chosen to characterize himself.

It is the overabundance of these things that has brought such confusion and chaos to our nation and indeed the world. We could work our way through some of it, but when it became the norm of mankind's mentality and conduct, we have become overwhelmed by it, and can no longer see a light at the end of the tunnel, so to speak. The problems have not changed thru the ages, but remain internal, in the mentalities of some of "our own countrymen" who have formed alliances against the Bible, its teachings, and those who teach it. As a result, our leaders are frustrated, the news media is frustrated, and consequently the people are driven to frustration, and confusion seems to reign supreme, especially in the ranks of the people who have rejected God's word of truth and absolutes. Yet in light of all this very obvious idiocy, these people will argue their pointless position exposing additional ignorance every time they speak.

I will refrain from opening any argument as to whether or not the redeemed community of Christ are any better than the unsaved, as [John 3: 16] points out that Christ died for all, of which we were all qualified as ungodly, [Romans 3: 23], " For all have sinned and come short of the glory of God". I am willing to leave that distinction between the saved and unsaved up to God as he separates the sheep from the goats, as who qualifies as a sheep versus a goat is entirely up to him, [Matthew 25: 32]. In the meantime, however we might consider [Acts 10: 34-35] as a point of interest and consideration by those who have eyes to see, ears to hear, and minds that are capable of comprehension and at least a little bit of understanding; "Then Peter open his mouth and said, of a truth

I perceive that God is no respecter of persons: BUT in every nation he that feareth him, and worketh righteousness, is accepted with him".

Having favor with God through meeting his Biblical directed requirements for such favor, and being accepted with him is a very comforting, and intelligent, position to be in. You may well get away with disagreeing with me, but to disagree with God will have some eternal devastating affects: I would suggest a path more in line with God's choosing. I would offer [Deuteronomy 30: 19] for intense consideration and study for beginners and as a refresher for the more advanced students, or just readers, of the bible.

Please don't get me wrong: I am not down on America, only the stupidity, ignorance, and overwhelming indulgence in sinful practices that has come to characterize American society, that is bringing about her ruin, and the idiots that promote and practice it; which is all within their "rights" of course. God created us to be intelligent beings, however, Adam cast that aside when he abdicated his dominion authority to Satan in the Garden of Eden, and man has been abdicating every since. Retained and exercised Godly intelligence would prevent the things that are bringing ruination, shame, and disgrace on our beloved America, but Godly intelligence and common sense seem to be non-existent in our nation these days along with other things mentioned in the Bible that are commensurate with righteous and holiness.

The question of, who is to blame, should prompt some interesting discussion and dialogue. Who knows, during the process, we might even discover the solution to many of our problems. As Christians, that should already be quite apparent. [Isaiah 5: 24], "Therefore as the fire devoureth the stubble, and the flame consumeth the chaff, so their root shall be as rottenness, and their flower shall go up as the dust: BECAUSE they have cast away the law of the Lord of hosts, and despised the word of the Holy One of Israel". The first portion of this scripture gives us a fair description of America if we don't get our spiritual act together. The latter portion gives us the result of excommunicating God and His Word by such things as "the separation of the church and state".

Then we have the remedy, [Mark 1: 15], "Repent and believe the gospel unto diligent obedience. This is a repeat of [2 Chronicles 7: 14], "If my people, which are called by my name, shall humble themselves, and pray, and seek my face, and turn from their wicked ways; then I will hear from heaven, and will forgive their sin, and will heal their land". There are a few more words used to emphasize this repentance essential, but the message is the same. [Deuteronomy 28] gives a very graphic difference between the people who dwell on the "If thou wilt hearken diligently" side of God's directions versus the unrepentant, "If thou wilt not hearken diligently" side in rebellion and disobedience. Consider this carefully.

Lacking the extended education that many of today's authors have, you may find my writings a bit rough around the edges for which I make no apology. This could prove an advantage in some ways as I don't have some things to unlearn as I progress and move ahead in my own studies. However, if we all stay with the same Bible for the purpose of unity, [John 17], and, to put in today's vernacular, "being on the same page", worshipping and serving the same God, creator of heaven and earth, the God of Israel, and diligently adhering to His counsel, we should remain fairly accurate as we progress, "seated together in heavenly places in Christ", [Ephesians 2: 4-10], continuing toward our eternal destiny of the kingdom of heaven while [Deuteronomy 28: 47], "serving the Lord our God with joyfulness, and with gladness of heart for the abundance of all things". This speaks of our attitude of service.

Though it seems that I may ramble a bit from time to time, it is my intention, whether I succeed or not, to present the readers with some Biblical truths and challenges they can get their "spiritual teeth into" for the purpose of growth, and development that they can apply toward Christian maturity, providing they are interested in doing so. If they are not so inclined, it is my prayer that some of these writings will induce enough curiosity to provide a challenge to compel them to additional studies, with my own writings and a multitude of others that are available to them. Let me challenge you to choose the books you read, and study, with wisdom and discretion, selecting only those that "add something to you" in the way of developing a Biblical, Christ like character, personality and attitude, "with the Word of God dwelling in you richly", [Colossians 3: 15-17], vs. 16.

You may find an occasional word misspelled for which I do apologize. Nevertheless, my main concern is that it is not spelled, or misspelled, so badly that it fails to contribute constructively to the message it is intended to convey. Allow me to assume my readers will have enough grace to overlook my errors and enough intelligence to get over the rough spots and around the chuck holes and capture the essence of these writings. May God richly bless you as we walk and learn together through my efforts to present God's truth and absolutes to you for counsel, guidance, and direction unto life and life more abundantly, giving glory, honor, and pleasure, to God, magnifying our Saviour Jesus, and edifying the body of Christ.

Although I am a fan of the Kings James Version, which I will use in the majority of my writing, I will not hesitate to refer to other Versions from time to time as occasionally I will find a word or phrase that seems more preferable to what needs to be said in order to get a better understanding of the message being given. An attempt will be made to identify the use of these various scriptures from the different versions with an explanation of why they are being used in preference to the K.J.V. By doing this it is hoped we can "stay on the same page".

You will notice the use of much scripture throughout my writing with several scriptures being used many times in various situations. You may criticize this as redundancy if you wish. We were all born critics and man has developed it to a fine art, whether it be constructive or destructive, which it is in most cases as man has only to allow his nature to take its natural course to do this. However, what some may view as redundancy in the often use and application of Biblical truths, I simply see as "emphasis" to be diligently applied as needed substance for Christian character and development in all our lives. May God give you additional understanding of his word every time you come into contact with it. May it be often and consistent; for emphasis and effect, of course.

As a conclusion to this introduction, allow me once again to go to the scriptures, [Hebrews 13: 20-21], "Now the God of peace, that brought again from the dead our Lord Jesus, that great shepherd of the sheep, through the everlasting covenant, Make you perfect in every good work to do his will, working in you that which is well pleasing in his sight, through Jesus Christ; to whom be glory for ever and ever. Amen. I look forward to meeting you in heaven, and possibly before.

Sincerely, in God's love
Darold F. Edwards

NOTES

ii. ACKNOWLEDGMENTS

I would like to thank the people who from the very beginning as a novice writer were kind enough to read some of my earliest efforts and gave me some very encouraging reviews. First of course I would like to thank God for guiding me into writing. It has become a real Godsend to me and has provided direction and purpose for me at a time when otherwise, retirement could have been very trying. I need purpose in my life and writing of the nature you will see in these books gave me that. During my electrical career when I was able to help build some material churches, I thought that someday I would like to assist in building the spiritual church of [Matthew 16: 18] in the hearts and lives of people. God has opened the door to do that through writing, for which I wish to express my soul depth gratitude.

Next, many heartfelt thanks to my dear wife Pat for encouraging me in everything along the way in our life together, what a strength and help she has been to me. Susan Canfield was one of the first, who has been very encouraging from the start. She also trims our Schnauzer, Max, which is another big help. This doesn't really have anything to do with my writing except it provides opportunity to visit with Susan from time to time to get additional input on the writing; she is always encouraging. Susan has been very helpful and encouraging in her comments and friendship. Thank you Susan.

Then there is Jock and Karen Elliot, some dear Christian friends who along with their family we have been blessed to know for many reasons including their encouragement in writing. Karen is also a great cook, which is another real advantage to knowing the right people, and I have been much blessed in this area by her talent. My son Myke is of an absolute necessity and blessing as he is my computer expert along with being my son and a very dear friend. I couldn't do this without him. Thanks Myke, for your ever patient and loving assistance along the way.

Then there is my dear friend and brother in the Lord, Clarence Parker, who comes over a couple of times a week just to talk, discuss, study Bible, and add his encouragement to me in my writing efforts. His comments are extremely uplifting and helpful. He also benefits from Karen's cooking, as do all who attend the Elliot's prayer meetings. What a great blessing and strength he is. Thank you my brother for standing alongside me during my writing struggles. Another dear friend, Nancy Gerling, has read some of my writings and has copies of my first efforts to have books published. She has always been extremely uplifting with her input concerning my writing. Many thanks to you, Nancy.

There are others that have added much to me with their encouraging comments about my works which are much appreciated. May God's blessings be upon them and may his presence fill their hearts and lives. May God's blessings also be added to you who are gracious enough to become a part of my reading public; let us study God's word together as he quickens us together in Christ, raises us up together, and makes us to sit together in heavenly places in Christ Jesus our Lord and Saviour, these places being made heavenly because of His presence, wherever that may be. May God's divine love abound in our hearts toward one another. Indeed; we do become a part of each other as we are a part of the body of Christ our Lord.

A little over a year ago as I was looking through a magazine advertising for a Restore America event, I run across another page where someone made the statement, **"How much information do we need before we get out of the boat and walk on the water"**. Whoever that person is, and wherever he may be, I would like to thank him for impacting my life with that inspirational word. Stepping out in faith and writing as I feel led of the Lord in my efforts is my way of walking on the water.

Your efforts are probably of a different calling than mine, but yet of the divine nature. May we blend our efforts and lives together in the unity Jesus prayed for in **John 17** for God's glory, honor, and pleasure. Come, walk with me as we journey along together with the multitudes who will join with us, as we all walk and sit together **"in heavenly places"**, inspiring each other as Jesus inspires us all. **To God be the glory forever and ever, Amen.**

NOTES

iii. PREFACE

[Ecclesiastes 12: 11-12], "The words of the wise are as goads, and as nails fastened by the masters of the assemblies, which are given from one Shepard. And further, by these, my son, be admonished: of making many books there is no end; and much study is a weariness to the flesh". Much study demands considerable self discipline, diligence and determination, and a lot of invested time, whereas simply reading for the enjoyment of what is being read, or other lesser purposes, without the element of **"study to show thyself approved unto God", [2 Timothy 2: 15],** tends to a great waste of time.

However, such is not the case if a time of relaxation from business or other things that tend to stress is needed, and reading a good book that is a "no brainer" may be just the ticket. Unfortunately this becomes the norm for many people. As a result many books that neither contribute anything of value and adding nothing constructive to the reader, are in great abundance and offer no challenge for growth and development. Unfortunately, these seem to be the norm and are in great demand. Consequently no study is required that would demand thought and concentration, so these books are read in pursuit of nothing, then put aside in favor of another "nothing" book or maybe just watching soap operas on T.V. or the equivalent in "nothing". Habits are thus formed with the result being wasted time and life. Non productive thinking and thought leads to a non productive, pointless existence, somewhat void of life and real living. This results in the term "they need to get a life", which applies to the worlds masses who are caught in the prison and bondage of earthly existence; **[Colossians 3: 2].**

Allow me to express extreme caution in the selection of your reading material as your reading is a direct input into the content of your mind and contributes heavily to "the abundance of your heart". So once again I say, proceed with wisdom, knowledge, understanding, and caution, applying some intelligence and plain common sense along the way, **[Proverbs 4: 23], "Keeping thy heart with all diligence; for out of it are the issues of life". [Proverbs 2: 11], "Discretion shall preserve thee; understanding shall keep thee".**

If we do not endeavor to establish our values and standards according to God's values and standards, we will exist in error continually without the life God has made available to us through Jesus Christ. It is with this in mind that I have set out to produce this work concerning the "RESURRECTION OF EXCELLENCY", with other writings and books following to challenge the readers, whoever or wherever they may be: to look inside themselves and ask intelligent questions about their being, who they are, what they are, how they came to be, their purpose, and what their eternal destiny is, and what it is comprised of and by God's design. I find it very enlightening to realize I have by "intelligent design" been created as a very special and unique being instead as a blob of something left to chance as claimed by some who are also willing to risk their eternal destiny with their continuing low level of an unchallenged demented mentality.

Don't think me uncaring and insensitive to others because I use words such as stupidity, idiocy, and ignorant at times. We have all been there and if we are not careful and conscientious about our Christian training, have a tendency to revert back to old habits from time to time. I have nothing against man; only against the inadequate mentalities they have chosen to victimize themselves with. Even as Christians, former erroneous habits and desires, at times even with God's assistance, are hard to shake and it takes time, perseverance and diligence to cast them aside and grow out of them. They may or may not be classified as sin in all cases, but regardless consist of things that do not "please the Lord," [John 8: 29], or "accompany salvation," [Hebrews 6: 9]. But in any event we need to [2 Timothy 2: 15], **"Study to show ourselves approved unto God, workmen that needeth not to be ashamed, rightly dividing the word of truth."** This involves the extensive effort of [Romans 12: 2] **"being transformed by the renewing of the mind", "exercising thyself unto Godliness",** [1Timothy 4: 7].

The displacing of these life destroying discrepancies will only be accomplished with the diligent study and input of God's Word. These are just simply some destructive traits of humanity that if not addressed and dealt with according to God's counsel, will continue to plague their unsuspecting, unknowledgeable victims regardless of whether or not they are saved. The devil is not choosey who he victimizes and he will use any method at his disposal to re-devour anyone who becomes negligent in the **"keeping of the heart with all diligence", [Proverbs 4: 23].** Remember, as a Christian, you are his prime target, you are his priority. All others are already devoured. Such is the result of disregarding God's counsel and direction to **"choose life and blessing rather than remaining in a state of death and cursing"** [Deuteronomy 30: 19].

I have had to reject the traditional terminology of "sinner saved by grace" in favor of **"a new creature in Christ, saved by Grace", [2 Corinthians 5: 17].** The reason for this was because the term "sinner" was not conducive to being [1 John 1: 7-9], **"forgiven of sin and cleansed from all unrighteousness by the blood of Jesus."** This is an insult to the power of the blood of Jesus to thoroughly cleanse from sin and unrighteousness in the name of Jesus for complete cleansing, forgiveness, deliverance and reconciliation. All this of course, is based on the condition of genuine, soul depth, repentance of sin and a commitment to **"fear [reverence] the Lord and work righteousness"** [Acts 10: 35], serving the

Lord with joyfulness and with gladness of heart, for the abundance of all things, [Deuteronomy 28: 47]. You may not agree with me on this issue and that's not important. Just be in agreement with God. It's his word that counts, not mine.

After all that God has done for us through Jesus Christ our Lord and Saviour in obtaining the **"divine nature of God through his great and precious promises", [2 Peter 1:2 -4],** it seemed that the title and name of "sinner" had some rather antagonistic and invasive qualities and connotations about it that never belonged nor fit in well with being **"a new creature in Christ saved by grace".** The term "sinner" always suggested being stuck in a rut with no incentive to move on, whereas the new distinction and a new attitude concerning being "a new creature in Christ" provides a glorious challenge to, **[1 Peter 1: 13], "Gird up the loins of our [spiritual] minds"** and, **[Hebrews 6: 1-3], "go on unto perfection"**, to the **[Job 4: 21], "Resurrection of the Excellency" which is in you, lest ye die, even without wisdom."**

NOTES

NOTES

I. MY FATHERS BUSINESS

[Luke 2:49] "And he said unto them, how is it that ye sought me? Wist ye not that I must be about *MY FATHERS BUSINESS*"? Approximately twenty-one years later he was to say in [John 17: 4] as he was praying to his Father concerning this business, **"I have glorified thee on the earth: I have finished the work that thou gavest me to do". In [John 14:12]** we are given some important insight into where we stand in relationship to the *"FATHERS BUSINESS"*. Jesus said **"Verily, verily, I say unto you, He that believeth on me, the works that I do shall he do also; and greater works than these shall he do; because I go unto my Father"**. It would certainly seem that Jesus left us some of the *FATHERS BUSINESS* to complete. Jesus completed what he was sent to do; I am afraid we, however, have not done nearly as well concerning our portion of the **"*Fathers Business*"**.

Could there be a depth of meaning concerning the **"believing on Jesus"** unto the business of **"doing these *greater works*"** that we just don't understand? I am convinced that the more we realize our inadequacies and failures in accomplishing what God has given us to do in our individual *"AREA OF SERVICE"*, the more we will appreciate the ever-present, always on the job, **"amazing Grace of God"** that takes up the slack for us. We can be geographically where God wants us, we can be physically executing the calling placed on us. We can seemingly have all our spiritual ducks in line with a great show of piety. On the surface, we look good. **[1 Samuel 16:7],"But the Lord said unto Samuel, Look not on his countenance, or the height of his stature; because I have refused him: for the Lord seeth not as man seeth; for man looketh on the outward appearance,** *but the Lord looketh on the heart"*.

This heart condition, *"STATE OF THE HEART* "that is demanded by God in service to Him is absent **[Deuteronomy 28: 45-47]**. Verse 45 gives the reasons for the curses, verse 46, the stigma attached to Israel because of them. In verse 47, we see additional reasons for the curses; **Because thou *servest not the Lord thy God* "with a proper attitude, a correct state of the heart;** the necessity of an overall **"attitude of willing obedient service"** borne out of a love desire to **"do always those things that please Him" [John 8: 29], "serving Him with joyfulness, and with gladness of heart for the abundance of all things"**, the example set by Jesus and commanded throughout God's word to **"Love the Lord thy God with all thy heart, soul, mind, strength, etc". "For in Him we live and move and have our being", [Acts 17:28].**

Jesus further emphasizes this in **[John 4:32], "But he said unto them, I have meat to eat to eat that ye know not of"**, the substance of which you have no understanding. Again in verse **34, "My meat is to do the will of Him that sent me, and to finish His work"**. Could Jesus be emphasizing here for our teaching, benefit, and example that in keeping with **[Acts 17:28]** above, that in His Father, he indeed **"lived and moved and had his total substance of being"**. His "meat" was his strength, his sustenance, his hearts desire, his total will, His life and life more abundantly; He was "wrapped up" in His Father. His love for His Father demanded this and Jesus, being constrained by His love for His Father, had to obey this love's desire to fulfillment. This demands study, meditation, work, and practice on our part, also for fulfillment.

It does appear that from the general condition of the world that we are living in the last days of this age as spoken of in various places in the Bible, and from that same general condition it is apparent that there is much left to be done. Could I have done more, and done it better, undoubtedly; could we all have done more, still, undoubtedly. Things have gotten terribly out of hand in our world in every way imaginable, primarily because we, humanity in general, past as well as present, allowed them to first to get out of hand in our own individual lives. Now the question arises; are we going to repent of our negligence of **[Colossians 3:2]**, **"setting our affection on things above"**, the negligence of loving, studying, and applying God's word and stirring up ourselves **[Isaiah 64: 9]** to take hold of him, or continue on with business as usual with **"the affections set on the things of earth"**?

I have heard it said that, "confession is good for the soul". There is much that goes into this such as soul depth repentance of sin. Without a scripture that specifically states this in just these words, there are many individually and collectively which certainly command, imply and prove this for confessing sins to the Father and **"and faults one to another" [James 5: 16]**, **"and pray for one another, that ye may be healed"**. Included in this process of confession there are a few things that are absolutely necessary in the day to day living of a victorious Christian life. To begin with, one must be honest enough with themselves to admit to themselves that they have some things that need to be confessed, repented, and cleansed of. These may not be gross sin to begin with but we are reminded in God's word that **[1 Corinthians 5:6; Galatians 5:9], "A little leaven leaveneth the whole lump"**. Even a small stain on the pure white garment of righteousness becomes, or evolves into, quite and issue if it is not recognized and repented of for cleansing.

Next we come to the point of humbling ourselves before God and each other and swallowing our pride, **[James 5:16]**, **"Confessing our faults one to another, and praying one for another that we may be healed"**. Here is where we get to an area that reveals to us whether or not we've gotten rid of all our pride, or at least a sufficient amount of it that will allow us to venture into this confession area, or if there is enough of this residual garbage hidden away in a corner of our attitude to mess us up. There was a book came out several years ago titled, "I'm Okay, Your Okay". I never read this book; there are a great many that I have never read, and have no desire to do so. I have read some very good inspirational books and some "others" that to quote Paul in **[Galatians 2:6], "they added nothing to me"**, and were promptly shelved, some without even being finished.

The book just mentioned seemed to have the idea of bolstering the self-esteem while contributing nothing to the building and development of character such as the cleansing that occurs through the confession process with all that is involved in it. This inflation of the self-esteem without meaningful contributions to the character is somewhat of a deceptive oxymoron. Character development in Jesus unto righteousness and holiness for the glory, honour, praise, and pleasure of God is really what life is all about, the **"cleansing of the inner man unto righteousness and holiness that the exterior may be clean also" [Matthew 23: 26]. [Romans 12:2], "Be not conformed to this world: but be ye transformed by the renewing of your mind, that ye may prove what is that good, and acceptable, and perfect will of God"**. This is the process with the results stated in **[Psalms 103: 2], "Bless the Lord, O my soul, and forget not all his benefits"**.

I've got a friend, Ned Goldman, who told me a story about a little colored lady who got up in a testimony service to use this scripture as a testimony; here's how it came out, **"Bless de Lawd O my soul, and I gets all de benefits"**. I can't guarantee the story as actually having taken place but I do believe I could guarantee the truth and accuracy of the statement even if there was a slight difference in the quotation. I wonder if God smiled when he heard that and wished all his children could get a hold of that fact and live accordingly. We either live with this truth in our hearts and speak out of the abundance of it, honoring

God with both lips and heart, or **"honour him with lips when the hearts are far from him", [Matthew 15:8; Mark 7:6]**. I believe the Bible terminology for this condition would be found in **[Matthew 23:27],"for ye are like whited sepulchers, which indeed appear beautiful outward, but are within full of dead men's bones and of all uncleanness"**.

It is quite easy to fall into these traps of the wisdom of this world in which we are born and conditioned from day one, unless we are blessed with some very vigilant, perceptive, Bible orientated parents and friends to get us off on the right foot, so to speak. Even then it is important for us as individuals to learn to **[Colossians 3:2], "Set our affection on things above, and not on things on the earth"**. Good parents, good friends, and *good government,* all themselves being Biblically grounded, will teach, encourage and assist in this growing in the grace of God process and virtually guaranteeing a strong and successful nation. Unfortunately when it comes to the spiritual aspect, which is the strength of the nation, our government comes up extremely short in meeting their obligations, requirements, and responsibilities. But then again, they are not the only ones guilty of this. Many of those, other than in governmental positions, in whose hands Jesus left the "*Fathers Business*" haven't really done a bang up job either. On the one hand we have the contrary elements, "our own *COUNTRYMEN*", of our nation that have degraded it, and on the other hand, we have the ones who stood by and watched it happen and in some cases used the Bible as an excuse for doing so.

I'm afraid we have not kept our hearts with all diligence as commanded in **[Proverbs 4:23]**; consequently there are times when the life that they were to issue forth did not materialize and we allowed the devil to get an advantage. Repentance and confession does seem to be rather an on-going situation. I guess this is an area where the **"baptism of repentance "[Mark 1:4;**

Acts 13:24] would be appropriate for a contribution to this character development spoken of earlier. Vigilance and diligence, two treasures that often get stored away in the attics of our minds to collect the cobwebs and dust of time, quite often become forgotten in the hustle and bustle of daily living and then we wonder why, **[Job 5: 7], the trouble that man is born unto as the sparks fly upward becomes a way of life,** and The *Fathers Business* goes on the back burner, quite unintentionally, of course. This back burner position of The *Fathers Business* is an effect that has many causes, usually under a common heading of, "sin", in at least one of its multitude of manifestations. This is due to the mind being conformed to this world, distracted by its thinking, ways and methods, which are all causes having, in most cases, very undesirable and quite often disastrous results and effects.

Thus we are commanded and again reminded in **[Romans 12:2], "And be not conformed to this world: but be ye transformed by the renewing of your mind, that ye may prove what is that good, and acceptable, and perfect will of God".** This learning, remembering, renewing and refocusing of our minds unto righteousness is of an absolute necessity, for with the mind we think, make our choices, and form our thought patterns, our concepts and perceptions, which translate into our ways and lifestyles. **[Isaiah 55:8-9], "For my thoughts are not your thoughts, neither are your ways my ways, saith the Lord. For as the heavens are higher than the earth, so are my ways higher than your ways, and my thoughts than your thoughts".**

This gives us quite a large area, even as Christian's, including some who think they know it all already, to grow into and develop into that which is pleasing to God. Thus in **[Revelation 4:11]** we find that though we were created, past tense, we are being, present tense, today, tomorrow, and for the rest of our lives, re-created by submission to God into that which is pleasing to him. Rest assured this, submission to God, must precede any expected or contemplated "re-creation". Get comfortable with His word, learn to delight in it, meditate on it, study it, and love it, for you will spend the rest of your time on this earth in God's rebuilding shop, and the more you get involved with the rebuilding, re-creating process, experience the benefits and rewards thereof, becoming aware of the immense value therein, the more you will desire to be like Jesus our Lord and Saviour.

Life is good, Life is interesting and exceedingly rewarding **"for it is in Him, our Lord, that we have life an life more abundantly, [John 10: 10]. It is in Him that we live and move and have our being, [Acts 17:28].** Without Him, some sort of survivalistic existence is all you can hope for in this world without even something good enough to be called an existence in your eternal destiny. **[Hebrews 11:6], "But without faith it is impossible to please him: for he that cometh to God must believe that he is, and that he is a rewarder of them that diligently seek him".** Here is that treasure of diligence that often gets stuck in the recesses of our "out of sight out of mind", the subconscious, only to be resurrected when some extraordinary, usually threatening, event shakes it loose.

We find in **[1 Peter 5:8]** a command to, **"Be sober, be vigilant; [then the reason for the command], because your adversary the devil, as a roaring lion, walketh about seeking whom he may devour".** Here are found two of the "attic of the mind treasures" of the whole counsel of God, along with "sobriety" added. Let's combine these "treasures" and see what we come up with in reference to the preceding scripture, which now may read, **"Exercise diligence in your sobriety with vigilance, and the keeping of your heart and mind with all God's counsel, because your adversary the devil, as a** roaring lion, walketh about seeking whom he may devour". I do wish the Bible translators would have translated this last line of this scripture *"as a deceitful snake, slithering about, seeking whom he may deceive and devour.* This would fit the devil's evil insidious character and nature more so than a "roaring lion" announcing his presence, thus warning us of his evil intentions. God himself has and is warning us of all this chaos and destruction if we rebel in union with this devil, and still the multitudes remain in rebellion, rejection, and disobedience.

Be assured, if you are a Christian, you are his target, if you are not a Christian, but are dead in your trespass and sins, you are already devoured. You were born devoured, **[Psalms 51:5], "Behold, I was shapen in iniquity; and in sin did my mother conceive me". [Ephesians 2:4-10], "BUT GOD, who is rich in mercy, for his great love wherein he loved us, even when we were dead in sins, hath quickened us together with Christ, [by grace are ye saved;] And hath raised us up TOGETHER, AND HATH MADE US SIT TOGETHER IN HEAVENLY PLACES WITH CHRIST JESUS: That in, and throughout, the ages to come he might show the exceeding riches of his grace in his kindness toward us through Christ Jesus. For by grace are ye saved through faith; and that not of yourselves: it is the gift of God: Not of works, lest any man should boast; For we are his workmanship, created in Christ Jesus unto good works, which God hath before ordained that we should walk in them".**

You don't have to understand it to benefit from it and enjoy it, but you do have to **"repent and believe the gospel", [Mark 1: 15],** unto obedience of its principles. You will learn and understand more as you grow in the grace and knowledge of our Lord and Saviour Jesus Christ. Here is another treasure that often is never developed or discovered: **"patience"**, be patient with others and yourself. This is a toughie to learn and come by as it is not normally something that is either taught or exercised in the world system to which we have all been overly exposed, thus conditioned. Even the church world has a tussle with this one. Many are the problems caused by a lack of patience. It reminds me of a message on a coffee cup, **"Give me patience Lord, but hurry"**

[Ephesians 2: 4], "But God, However, God, Nevertheless, God, who through Jesus Christ hath redeemed us and reconciled us to himself, even when we were dead in sins, and very likely without patience, hath quickened us together with Christ, [by grace are ye saved"]. Be patient with yourself lest you become discouraged and fall by the wayside, devoured by the adversary. Be patient with yourself in your efforts and time to learn and apply Biblical principles and truth. But be exceedingly diligent in your pursuit of such wisdom, knowledge, understanding, and the intelligence to perceive such, **[Matthew 6:33],** in the establishment of life, as worthy of your time, effort, and energies and the common sense to apply it as light is received along your journey of learning, growing and developing; in being **[Revelation 4:11]** re-created by God's own hand.

The glorious majesty and immensity of it is far beyond the ability of attainment in one lifetime, but the choice to repent and believe the gospel unto obedience is but a momentary event even though the Holy Spirit has been dealing with you about it for a considerable length of time. So be patient with yourself and your brethren in your learning and developing process. Give the Holy Spirit, this divine teacher and educator of heaven, the time and opportunities he will need to get through the obstinacy we have been influenced and conditioned with by this world to open our hearts and minds to the truth of the gospel and understanding of it. Be prepared, be patient, be diligent: it will take time, but the rewards of perseverance are beyond our comprehension and absolutely majestic.

Be patient, be understanding, in your diligence. Your opposition may be some of your own household; many will be of your own countrymen. Continue in patience and well doing and the love and nurturing of God in his many manifestations and methods of tender, loving care and encouragements. Be kind, considerate, and understanding toward those that oppose you, they are only walking where you walked in your own times of opposition and disobedience. Pray for them, that their eyes of understanding will be opened to the gospel. However, remain steadfast and immovable in the gospel of God's truth and the absolutes it presents, being faithful unto death. Unto this have we all been called, this is OUR FATHERS BUSINESS. As such, it must be our priority.

NOTES

NOTES

II. JESUS OUR HOPE

[Matthew 10:34-39], "Think not that I am come to send peace on earth: I came not to send peace, but a sword. For I am come to set a man at variance against his father, and the daughter against her mother, and the daughter in law against her mother in law. And a man's foes shall be they of his own household. He that loveth father or mother more than me is not worthy of me: and he that loveth son or daughter more than me is not worthy of me. And he that taketh not his cross and followeth after me, is not worthy of me. He that findeth his life shall lose it: and he that *loseth his life for my sake* shall find it". This is expanded further in **[2 Corinthians 11:26]** where Paul speaks of **"being in perils of mine own countrymen"**. Again in **[1 Thessalonians 2:14]**, **"For ye, brethren, became followers of the churches of God which in Judea are in Christ Jesus: for ye also have suffered like things of "your own countrymen"**, [possibly some even of your own households] **even as they have of the Jews"**.

There is another approach to this portion of scripture concerning the "losing of life for God's sake and finding it" that needs to be brought into focus here for deep consideration, as it includes the very basis of all sin and is so subtle that it is seldom thought of as such. This is the matter of **"selfishness"**. Lucifer, Satan, the devil, call him as you wish, manifested this when he wanted God's position and power for himself. There is the element of **"covetousness"** also included in this that we must be aware of. All of this is all inclusive of the life that in operation exhibits some additional evil tendencies that must be **"lost for my sake in order to find it"**. The arrogant announcement of the world that "I have my rights" is somewhat reminiscent and suggestive of this selfishness and covetousness that is so characteristic of, and plagues humanity.

It is always present and in operation when God's commandment to **"choose life so that both thou and thy seed both may live", [Deuteronomy 30: 19],** is rejected: death and cursing being the result of such foolishness and idiocy. Much is needed here in the practice of **[2 Timothy 2: 15],** concerning the intense study of God's principles to get a personal understanding of what is taking place in all of this, the development of the life unto a Christlike character, **[2 Corinthians 10: 5] "Casting down *vain* imaginations, and every high thing that exalteth itself against the knowledge of God, and bringing into captivity every thought to the obedience of Christ".**

There are many, who of the past and multitudes in the present, that are "of our own countrymen and of our own households that are our "foes" simply because they are opposed to the gospel of Jesus Christ and reject its message of life and life more abundantly. Thus they are not only enemies of Christ, and our foes, but *"oppose themselves"*. **[2 Timothy 2:25-26], "In meekness instructing those that *oppose themselves*; if God peradventure will give them repentance to the acknowledging of the truth; And that they may *recover themselves* out of the snare of the devil, who are taken captive by him at his will".** The "recovering of themselves" is mentioned again in **[Acts 2:40], "And with many other words did he testify and exhort, saying, *save yourselves from this untoward generation*".**

The method for this is taught throughout the Bible and is based on each and every individual simply making an intelligent, correct "choice". This choice is directly commanded in **[Deuteronomy 30:19], "I call heaven and earth to record this day against you, that I have set before you life and death, blessing and cursing, therefore CHOOSE life, that both thou and thy seed may live".** Again in **[Mark 12:15], "The time is fulfilled, and the kingdom of God is at hand:**

[choose to] repent and believe the gospel" [unto salvation and obedience].

Among these that oppose God, his word and message, and thus oppose themselves, we find organized groups as well as individuals that function and attempt to conceal themselves under the title and guise of "church" while others are very vocal and aggressive in their opposition to the gospel of God, **[Isaiah 5:24] "casting his word behind their backs and despising the word of the Holy One of Israel",** and the opposition continues with the **[Matthew 15:14; Luke 6:39] blind leaders leading the deceived blind followers, and all struggling along** [in their deceptive blindness on] **the [Matthew 7:13] broad way that leads to the ditch of destruction.**

To serve a group, secular organization, or even a seemingly religious organization without serving God and man, is to be counted among those that are trapped on this broad road of blindness to destruction. Christ is our hope, humanity's only hope, of deliverance from this world's destructive influence and conditioning. It is possible, and often happens, to get so involved in the business of the workings, management, and enforcement of denominational rules, regulations, and requirements, that intimacy with God is lost or never really attained to. This results in **[Matthew 15: 8], "This people draweth nigh unto me with mouth, and honoureth me with their lips; but their heart is far from me".**

[John 10:10], "The thief cometh not but for to steal, and to kill, and to destroy: I am come that they might have life, and that they might have it more abundantly". If you have no peace in your life, it is because you have been conned into living a lifestyle that does not produce peace. Thus the thief has successfully and deceitfully stolen your peace. If you have no hope of a better future than what you have been experiencing, it is because you have placed your confidence in the world and not in Jesus; you have been following deceptive **"ungodly counsel" [Psalms 1:1], "the wisdom of this world which is foolishness with God", [1Corinthians 1: 20; 3:19],** and not "the counsel of God". Consequently the thief has killed your hope. Now you are left without peace or hope. To be without one or the other is disastrous, but to have neither one is totally destructive. A common, well known symptom of this is what is called "depression" which is a result of an over abundance of what is common unto man, "worry", **"being overcharged with the cares of this life",** among other things we should not indulge in, **[Luke 21:34].** All this being worried, depressed, and despondent *is a result of losing, or never developing confidence in, and trusting God, committing your ways to the Lord and allowing him to direct your paths,* **[Proverbs 3: 5-6]**.

The world has some fancy names for all this, but it all stems from **"no knowledge of God", [Hosea 4:6], the sin of unbelief;** no trust or confidence in God to assist us in getting us through the problems of life **"and the weight and sin that doth so easily beset us", [Hebrews 12:1].** There is no escaping all the problems of this world, *but through a Biblical orientated lifestyle* you can prevent a great many of them and be guided safely through the ones you can't escape, **[Psalms 23].** If by some miracle you managed to evade causing your own, there are people around, **"of your own household, or countrymen"**, that will make sure you don't miss out entirely.

However, being human, even as a Christian, you will very naturally cause enough of your own to keep you busy trying to find and apply solutions, wherein we usually manage to cause more problems because we fail to initiate the correct solutions, or the solution Himself, and once again, God has to bail us out. **[Job 5: 6-7], "Although affliction cometh not forth of the dust, neither doth trouble spring out of the ground; Yet man is born unto trouble as the sparks fly upward". [Isaiah:**

50:11], **"Behold, all ye that kindle a fire that compass yourselves about with sparks: walk in the light of your fire, and in the sparks that ye have kindled. This shall ye have of mine hand; ye shall lie down in sorrow"**. Judgment and trouble are a natural result of kindling the sparks of rebellion and disobedience that quite often grow into full fledged fires of chaos and destruction, whether caused by our own hand or others.

Most of us human beings, even as Christians; are not immune to problems, having experienced considerable difficulties in our days, some more than others. I don't care for problems and difficulties and have made a study of how to avoid many of them, or at least not cause them myself. I do, however, slip up occasionally. I will have to admit, I have experienced streaks of dumb from time to time, but lay no claim to embracing a constant state of utter stupidity which seems to characterize our present post modern world. I have developed a particular hunger for God's word and the nourishment for the mind, heart, and soul that I find there that as a natural result provide much peace, joy, comfort, and happiness, plus many other advantages that are mentioned throughout God's Word. **[Psalms 119:165],"Great peace have they that love thy law, word, and nothing shall offend them, or be a stumbling block, to them"**. This world has deceived me in all its manipulations, maneuverings, and scheming, and there is no room there to place trust or confidence. I do wish I had learned this at a much earlier age; but older more experienced eyes see things that younger eyes are oblivious to, **[Proverbs 4: 7], "Wisdom is the principle thing; therefore get wisdom: and with all thy getting *get understanding*"**.

There are a few advances wherein mans endeavors have proved fruitful in what has been accomplished. For instance: I would much prefer to cut a winters supply of firewood with a good chainsaw than an old fashioned crosscut saw. Been there, done that, and have no desire to go back. We would no doubt agree that to take a trip in a nice comfortable car is much to be preferred to a horse and buggy. There are on the other hand, in spite of good intentions, many that have been disastrous even though to some degree successful. All are eventually doomed to failure for mans sinful oriented nature does nothing to bring glory to God, but only to himself. Thank God for the exceptions.

Man in his sinful, unregenerate state is described in **[Isaiah 64:6-7], "But we are all as an unclean thing, and all our righteousnesses are as filthy rags; and we all do fade as a leaf; and our iniquities, like the wind, have taken us away. And there is none that calleth upon thy name;** *that stirreth up himself to take hold of thee:* **for thou hast hid thy face from us, and hast consumed us, because of our iniquities".**

It continues with a wonderful manifestation of God's love in **[Ephesians 2:1-10], "And you hath he quickened, who were dead in trespass and sins; Wherein ye walked in times past according to the course of this world, according to the prince of the power of the air, the spirit that now worketh in the children of disobedience: Among whom we all had our conversation in times past through the lusts of the flesh, fulfilling the desires of the flesh and of the mind; and were by nature the children of wrath, even as others. BUT GOD, who is rich in mercy, with his great love wherewith he loved us, EVEN when we were dead in sins, hath quickened us together with Christ, [by grace are ye saved;] And hath raised us up TOGETHER, and made us sit TOGETHER in heavenly places [TOGETHER] in Christ Jesus. That in, [and throughout] the ages to come he might show the exceeding riches of his grace in his kindness toward us through Christ Jesus. For by grace are ye saved through faith; and that not of yourselves: it is the gift of God: Not of** works, lest any man should boast. For we are his workmanship; created in Christ Jesus unto good works, which God hath before ordained that we should walk in them"**. Unfortunately, the modern church has lost much of this wonderful unity of **"togetherness in Christ"** that used to feed our souls and spirits and strengthen the bond of being family among us.

One of the scriptures that expresses the beauty of "being and dwelling together" stands out by the use of the word **"unity"**, **[Psalms 133:1], "Behold, how good and how pleasant it is for brethren to dwell together in unity"**. Unfortunately, we often experience "brethren" in physical proximity to each other, but not **"dwelling together in unity"** of Biblical direction. This is one of the "gates of hell" that the church is guilty of raising against itself, and often prevailing without the church even realizing it. The contention that causes this is the product of hearts that are not diligently kept and minds still in conformity to some worldly ways of selfishness, deception, and other areas of error. This is neither good nor pleasant and does not glorify God nor the person and name of Jesus. It only brings shame and disgrace on the church, and is a blight on the whole of Christianity.

This is what Jesus wanted to prevent when in **[John 17]** he prayed so earnestly for the unity of the brethren, the church; that we might dwell together in unity with each other and with Him, using Himself and his Father and the unity which they experienced as a model. This is another area where we have not done very well, and in some areas and churches quite poorly as a matter of fact. We can't lay the blame for this on the world as it originates within the church. **[Psalms 127: 1], "Except the Lord build the house, they labor in vain that build it"**. Is it any wonder that Jesus announced in **[Matthew 16: 18]** that he was going to build his own church distinctly different from the ones men had built, one against which the gates of hell could not prevail. He is still building it today in the hearts and lives of his sincere, committed followers whoever the may be and wherever they are found. **[Acts 10: 34-35], "Then Peter opened his mouth and said, Of a truth I perceive that God is no respecter of persons:** *But in every nation he that feareth him, and worketh righteousness, is accepted with him"*.

Man in his unregenerate, sinful, spiritually dead state, was totally without hope of deliverance or rescue from that condition of "deadness", bound for a devils hell for eternity: But an intervening, loving, merciful God, **[Ephesians 2: 4-10]**, stepped in with a correct solution, the only solution possible to the otherwise eternal destiny in hell that awaited the sinning soul, and still awaits the unrepentant sinner. **[I Peter 1: 3-4], "Blessed be the God and Father of our Lord Jesus Christ, which according to his abundant mercy hath begotten us again unto a lively hope by the resurrection of Jesus Christ from the dead, To an inheritance incorruptible, and undefiled, and that fadeth not away, reserved in heaven for you"**. But God through Christ Jesus, the answer and the solution, provided salvation, redemption, and reconciliation to the lost, the dead, the hopeless: a solution that was so complete and powerful, that if one availed themselves of that which was made available to them, would transform the sinner into a **[2 Corinthians 5:17] new creature in Christ [saved by the amazing grace of God]**.

I am reminded of that old hymn with the line in it, **"I was once [past tense] a sinner, but I came, pardon to receive from my Lord; now I am forgiven, and I know that he always keeps his word. There's a new name written down in glory, and it's mine, oh yes it's mine, with my sins forgiven I am bound for heaven, never more to roam"**. And another one: **"Redeemed, how I love to proclaim it, redeemed by the blood of the Lamb, redeemed by his** infinite mercy, his child and forever I am". **It is good to be "a new creature in Christ saved by the amazing grace of God, with even the old title of "sinner" washed away. How wonderfully powerful is this cleansing blood of Jesus.**

Gone forever is this old sinner concept, including the depressing, condemning title that provided no challenge to improve. I see it as an insult to the name and blood of Jesus, after all he has done to redeem and reconcile us back to God, to retain the title of "sinner saved by grace" when he has provided a new title "a new creature in Christ saved by grace" position for us. The whole idea is for us as individuals to make certain we are "in Christ" which challenges us to learn **God's way of thinking so our ways become according to his ways, [Isaiah 55:8]**. This becomes easier as we learn to **[Psalms 1:2], "delight in God's word and meditate in it day and night"**. Then we become, as we grow in grace and knowledge, like the person described in **verse 3, "And he shall be like a tree planted by the rivers of water that bringeth forth his fruit in his season: his leaf also shall not wither and whatsoever he doeth shall prosper"**. We must exercise ourselves to get a *vision of the values* in **"diligently seeking and serving God with joyfulness and gladness of heart for the abundance of all things", [Deuteronomy 28: 47]**.

Religion, as such, must be excluded from state and governmental functions; reason, there are many concepts, philosophies, convictions, etc., that comprise the many and various religions of this world that contradict each other to the point of disagreement and violent warfare among men. Not only do they contradict each other, they all contradict and are opposed to the Christian "religion", or faith in many ways, beginning with the deifying and worshipping of one or more false "gods" and the rejection of Jesus as the Son of God and the Messiah. This being said, the Christian Religion alone,

God's provision with it's principle's and precept's, the Bible teachings which were, and still should be, the strength of America, must by necessity for the survival and life of the nation, form the standards and values by which this nation or any nation can hope to grow, develop, and prosper.

Reject, and, or neglect the execution of those Godly values and standards in the operation, management, and function of an individual person or nation, and certain deterioration unto death immediately commences.**[Psalms 53: 1], "The fool hath said in his heart, there is no God". "The gift of God is still life and the wages of sin is still death", [Romans 6: 23]**. These two absolutes have not, nor can they ever change. God has not changed his mind or agenda concerning sin, the wages of which, still remains, the same. These Bible established principles are every bit as much a responsibility and obligation for the civil authorities to promote for the prosperity and well being of the nation they have pledged to uphold, protect and encourage as they are for the church leaders.

These leaders themselves, regardless of their positions or titles, were meant to be a part of the church to protect and encourage its Biblical teachings and further its standards and values for the glory of God and the prosperity of the nation and its people. As an example from the Old Testament: **[2 Kings 22: 1-2], "Josiah was eight years old when he began to reign, and he reigned thirty and one years in Jerusalem. And his mother's name was Jedidah, the daughter of Adaiah of Boscath.** *And he did that which was right in the sight of the Lord, and walked in all the way of David his father and turned not aside to the right hand or to the left"*.

No four year term for these old world leaders. If they were corrupt, they lead the people away from God into spiritual, psychological slavery and bondage which sooner or later resulted in physical, national slavery and bondage. Today we are saddled with their counterpart, our judges, some of which are appointed for a lifetime whether or not they are committed to obedience for the promotion and teaching of Gods word, which by all indications they seldom are, or are even concerned about. These people have usurped unlimited power of decision and policy making much to the detriment of the entire nation, and our elected leaders don't have the wherewithal to correct this ridiculous nation destroying situation. **[Isaiah 5: 20-21], "Woe unto them that call evil good, and good evil; that put darkness for light, and light for darkness; that put bitter for sweet and sweet for bitter! Woe unto them that are wise in their own eyes, and prudent in their own sight"**!

This is still God's world and his rules for the operation of it still apply. The "church" leaders and authorities have additional duties and responsibilities in "feeding the sheep", teaching, training, pasturing, etc. that the civil leaders may not have. There is however, a total lack of understanding that these "civil leaders" of our governmental structure were provided by God for the protection, nurture, and expansion of the church; never to create for themselves a separate entity from the church and become an opposition to it. Because of their failure in this, our nation has and is seeing history repeating itself as the likeness of **[Deuteronomy 28: 37]** is taking shape as are many other scriptures pertaining to judgments for rebellion and rejection of God and his Word, **[Ecclesiastes 1: 9-10].**

However due to the absolute necessity of the execution of Biblical Christian principles for the promotion of well being among the population of a nation, thus the nation, it becomes the duty and obligation of civil authorities to protect and advance these principles. Instead they have done quite the opposite in allowing and promoting diversity and tolerance of other religions and philosophies that are opposed to and destructive to the American Christian belief system which has afforded America divine protection. In doing so, they have signed America's death warrant.

Instead of protecting America from foreign evil invasion of destructive beliefs, concepts, practices, and philosophies, they have initiated America's destruction by inviting, welcoming, and making a home for the leaven which has contributed to the corruption of the whole. America, on its own, was doing quite well in this area and didn't need any foreign help. It is absolutely amazing that they attribute America's greatness to the establishment and execution of these actions. In an attempt to release themselves from their responsibility of the protection and promotion of God's established and ordained principles for the operation of this or any nation, his entire creation, they have initiated a constitutional decree of the "separation of church and state". Indeed, **"What fools ye mortals be"**!

This does not, however, release the civil entities from their God ordained duties and responsibilities as national leaders to encourage the following of the Bible principles that are the strength and foundation of America. The Christian populace must **"come out of its closet"** with boldness and courage, and demand this re-establishment of God's Word and his divine counsel for the management of this great nation or America will continue on its downward course of sin, iniquity, and degradation. The Christian community is going to have to exhibit a uniting, "unity" among themselves before the world will ever take them seriously. I'm concerned that the Christian community has taken this teaching of grace to the point where it is permissible to be insincere about obedience and commitment to Biblical principles because we are "saved by grace". Certainly this misuse and abuse of grace is displeasing to God and has a strong tendency to bring additional and continual disintegration into the Christian family, thus to our entire nation. We are certainly seeing the adverse effects of it throughout our population.

How can a light that has lost its glow and a salt that has lost its savor be affective any longer in their intended purpose? How can we expect a sinful society to take the Christian philosophy seriously when many of the Christians themselves have become so insincere and sloppy in its promotion and practice? Having abdicated dominion power and authority to the enemy, how can we as Christians expect to re-establish this authority when we have stood by and allowed the enemy to set rules, laws, and regulations against such re-establishment, thus having made the Christian religion and faith illegal while allowing that which is opposed to it free reign of promotion? Indeed has William Shakespeare said, and again I quote; "**What fools ye mortals be**". Ole Willie had us pretty well pegged, didn't he? It has gotten worse as time goes by, **[Hosea 4: 6-7], verse 7, "As they were increased, so they sinned against me: therefore will I change their glory into shame"**. The shame increases, and the glory is diminished.

Indeed we are saved by God's amazing grace, *but we live and move and have our being in Him, conducting ourselves in obedience to his divine principles of righteousness.* Consequently much of the professing Christian family have become very loose and sloppy in their concern and consideration about **"studying to show themselves approved unto God" [2 Timothy 2: 15], embracing and perfecting those "things that accompany salvation" [Hebrews 6:9]: "doing always those things that please God" [John 8: 29], and, "serving the Lord thy God with joyfulness and gladness of heart for the abundance of all things" [Deuteronomy 28: 47]**. *I see no reason or excuse to become defensive when we are attacked by groups and individuals who have nothing to offer as a viable option to the vastness of God's abundant supply and provisions*, but rather we must be pro-active in the declaration of proclaiming the truth of the gospel of Jesus Christ, the truth that sets men and nations free from the deceptions and bondage of their sins. The Christians **"have the truth, and the weapons of our warfare are not carnal, but mighty through God to the pulling down of strongholds", [2 Corinthians 10: 4].**

Let the opposition attempt to defend their position if they think they have conjecture worth defending. After all, what is their point? Their arguments go nowhere, point to nothing and prove even less with no benefits or reward for their maintaining their hopeless position. And who or what is available to reward them for their blindness in following the blind? Indeed, what reward could they possibly hope for? What possible advantage can there be for remaining blind to the life giving, delivering truth of God's word? **[Proverbs 1: 7], "The fear of the Lord is the beginning of knowledge: but fools** continue to **despise wisdom and instruction". [Psalms 14: 1], "The fool hath said in his heart, there is no God".**

The thief cometh not but for to steal, kill, and destroy, and he has worked his destruction by way of his deception in such a subtle way that those being stolen from, killed, and destroyed don't even realize it's taking place, but enjoying it as it is taking place. Such is the deception and pleasures of sin. **[Romans 1:22], "Professing themselves to be wise, they became fools"**, and will fight you for their "right" to remain fool's and continue on in their destructive thinking and ways, destroying themselves and their "seed". There is no wisdom, knowledge, understanding, intelligence, or common sense present in this manner of conduct and behavior. I feel I must quote Shakespeare here once again, **"What fools ye mortals be".** Are we so blind that we can't observe and learn from the bumps of idiocy on the other fellows head? We have to experience our own over and over again, and in many cases, still fail to learn obedience to God's principles, his word and Godly counsel of deliverance. **[Psalms 1: 1], "Blessed is the man that *walketh not in the counsel of the <u>ungodly</u>,* nor standeth in the way of** sinners, nor sitteth in the seat of the scornful". But his delight, his desire, is in the *Godly counsel of the word of the Lord*, and in His Word doth he meditate day and night". [John 8: 36], "If the Son therefore shall make you free, ye shall be free indeed".

I am seeing this more as time goes on, not only exterior to the "church" but within what used to be the church. The producing of "new versions" of the Bible, are not new versions at all, but are optional substitutions of some of the previous accepted versions. Please understand that I am not in any way discounting the good that is to be found in some of these versions, which good I also tap into occasionally. It does make it a bit difficult at times *"stay on the same page"* when there are many versions in a group gathered together for a study. Some, in their sad attempt to be "politically correct", so as not to offend anyone, have in their foolishness offended God himself by diluting and thus polluting his word with their humanistic non-sense.

When the Christian community has allowed the "political correctness" of a God rejecting state to infiltrate the church and dictate Biblical policy, in opposition to **"Biblical Correctness"** construction, and truth; then that community is well on it's way to ceasing to be "Christian community", and is dangerously like **[Hosea 4: 6-7]:** only in an advanced condition. Soul depth repentance is now desperately needed, in order, and soon, very soon. There may be a disagreement about whether or not **[Revelation 22:19]** applies to only the book of Revelation or to the whole Bible. It would be the height of foolishness to keep the book of Revelation intact while desecrating the rest of the Bible with errors and doing it intentionally for the sake of diversity and tolerance of that which is contrary to righteousness and holiness.

It does seem that the "Biblical brain deadness" of the world has taken quite a foothold in the church. The gates of hell are slamming shut, and I perceive, prevailing in many areas. **[Ecclesiastes 1:9-10], "The thing that hath been, it is that which shall be; and that which is done is that which shall be done: and there is no new thing under the sun. Is there any thing whereof it may be said; See, this is new? It hath been already of old time, which was before us".** Desecration, deceit, misuse, and abuse, have been attempted against God's truth since time began as we know it, beginning in the Garden of Eden and continued every since. Diluted, polluted truth which, by its very nature is no truth at all and is nothing new, neither are attempts to make it so. Man in his idiocy and pride still attempts to outwit God, and our world on the brink of destruction is testimony to that fact.

Is it any wonder that Jesus tells us in **[Matthew 16:16-18] that he is going to build his church on the rock of truth that he is indeed "the Christ, the Son of the Living God", and then declares that the "gates of hell shall not prevail against it".** It does seem as though he is making a definite distinction between "his church" and other churches not necessarily built by him. **[Psalms 127:1], "Except the Lord build the house, they labour in vain that build it, except the Lord keep the city, the watchman waketh but in vain".** The "gates of hell" are not always established directly by who we would normally consider as the thief, but by his willing slaves, many of our own countrymen, and some, unfortunately not just a few, having church membership.

Church problems and splits are much more caused by those within the church than by those outside of it. His henchmen are everywhere, including some wearing sheep's clothing, some intentionally, some unwittingly, carried away with their own lusts and ignorance, **"who are taken captive by him at his will",** [2 Timothy 2: 26]. [1Peter 5:8], "Be sober, be vigilant;

because your adversary the devil; as a roaring lion, walketh about seeking whom he may devour". [2 Corinthians 2:11], "Lest Satan should get an advantage of us: for we are not, or at least should not be, **ignorant of his devices"**. If we are ignorant of his devices, or at least a major part of them, we haven't done our homework nor have we inspired others to do theirs, and we are most vulnerable.

It does seem as though there are many who have been deceived, and have become very ignorant of his devices in our post-modern world and in some church's. **[1 Peter 4:17-18], "For the time is come that judgment must begin at the house of God: and if it first begin at us, what shall the end be of them that obey not the gospel of God? And if the righteous scarcely be saved, where shall the ungodly and sinner appear"?** It looks as though the ungodly and the sinners have a real problem ahead of them and they are not going to be able to hide, "assemble themselves together" within the "house of God" to escape this judgment, which is to begin at the house of God. Even having their names on the church roster will not suffice, **[Revelation 21:27], "but they which are written in the Lamb's book of life, those who keep their hearts with all diligence which issue forth life, those who delight and meditate day and night in God's word, those who study to show themselves approved unto God, those who set their affection on the things above and not on the things on earth, those who do always those things that please God, those who embrace and practice those things that accompany salvation"**. Familiarize yourselves with the scriptures references containing these last few lines, their location and the need for them in all our lives.

These are those who have discovered the immense, eternal, value of God's word and the counsel and fullness thereof; and it has become their passion, priority, and pursuit. These are they that have **developed the attitude of serving the Lord their God with joyfulness and gladness of heart for the abundance of all things.** This Almighty God has made his great abundance available to all through Jesus Christ, our Hope and our Blessed Assurance of Life and Life more Abundantly for today, tomorrow, and forever. To even think about believing in something or someone that is contrary to the promises, potential, and possibilities that are present in the person of Jesus Christ, our Saviour and Lord, is absolutely ludicrous and the epitome of foolishness.

Why take a chance on throwing in your lot with something or someone that leads nowhere, has no benefits or rewards, promises nothing, gets you out on a limb and promptly saws it off behind you? I would like to think that people are smarter than that, and exercise sufficient intelligence to avoid such things, but the signs and evidence prove otherwise for the bulk of humanity. There are of course, the exceptions that have without reservation, chosen the way of the cross of calvary that leads through the strait gate and on the narrow way that takes us home to life and life more abundantly. Intelligence is not non-existent; it is just that it resides in a select few who have made the correct choices and shown such intelligence by making those choices. **[Deuteronomy 30:19], "Therefore choose life, choose Jesus, the way of the cross, that both you and your seed, your children, your descendents, shall live".**

With all of God's provided abundance and fullness available, why take a chance on missing out on it when it is only a choice away. That is not intelligence, regardless of who you are and your station or position in this world. **[John 10:1-10], Vs.1, "Verily, verily, I say unto you, He that entereth not by the door into the sheepfold, but climb up some other way, the same is a thief and a robber. Vs. 7, Then said Jesus unto them again, Verily, verily, I say unto you, I am the door of the sheep. 8, All that ever came before me are** thieves and robbers: but the sheep did not hear them. 9, I am the door: by me if any man enter in, he shall be saved, and shall go in and out, and find pasture. 10; The thief cometh not but for to steal, and to kill, and to destroy; I am come that they might have life, and that they might have it more abundantly".

This idea that is so popular among the non-Christians, that all religious roads lead to heaven is a lie right out of the pits of hell and has proved, and is proving the downfall of many who fall for such deception disguised as love, relativity, tolerance, acceptance, etc. Those who promote such evil deceptions are most certainly the devil's advocates, and they may well be of your own household or countrymen.

We do have those among us who apparently know very little if anything of God's word that would like to think they are authorities on the subject and would like for others to believe it too. Regardless of who you are or what you believe, **"ye must be born again", [John 3:3-7].** There is no option to this. There are no other roads that lead to heaven: there are no other ways that lead to heaven. **[John 14:6], "Jesus saith unto him, I am the way the truth, and the life: no man cometh to the Father but by me". [Acts 4: 10-12], vs.12 "Neither is there salvation in any other: for there is none other name under heaven given among men, whereby we must be saved". [2 Peter 1: 2-15], "verse's. 10-11, "Wherefore the rather brethren, give diligence to make your calling and election sure: for if ye do these things, ye shall never fall: For so an entrance shall be ministered unto you abundantly into the everlasting kingdom of our Lord and Saviour Jesus Christ".**

It makes no difference what we think or don't think: all that counts is what God thinks, and he speaks what he thinks. All we have to do is be in obedient agreement with him, **[Matthew**

17:5; Mark 9:7; Luke 9:35], "And there came a voice out of the cloud, saying, This is my beloved Son in whom I am well pleased; hear ye him". Jesus is the hope, the only hope of mankind unto salvation, redemption, and reconciliation unto God, [Hebrews 11:6], "But without faith it is impossible to please him: for he that cometh to God must believe that he is, and that he is a rewarder of them that diligently seek him". [1Peter 1:13], "Wherefore, gird up the loins of your mind, be sober and hope to the end for the grace that is to be brought unto you at the revelation of Jesus Christ".

NOTES

NOTES

III. LOVE

If you think me to harsh in my depiction of the human race, please understand that I do not mean to categorize them because there are definitely exceptions to the norm of the general behavioral patterns we witness daily in our world, including America. With our news media and communications systems as they are today, biased and unbiased, the world in all its waywardness comes alive right in our own homes via the television, as we can watch events in progress around the world. Some of them are quite graphic portrayals of human behavior, but what else is to be expected from the masses who have, **[Isaiah 5:24], "cast away the law of the Lord of hosts and despised the word of the Holy One of Israel, his word of absolutes in the teaching of love, righteous, holiness, purity, goodness, etc, etc".**

All these conditions of the world with its war's, rumors of wars, chaos, confusion, famine, starvation, and the list goes on and on are all foretold in God's word, the Bible. There is not one prophesy in God's word that has not come to pass at its appointed time, with others left to come in their appointed time. It would be wise and a good show of intelligence to be aware of them and take the appropriate steps necessary in relationship to them. Please be advised, this world did not descend into the sinful, degraded, state that it is by the implementation of the Biblical principals of wisdom, knowledge, understanding, and Godly intelligence etc. Once again this was, and is, caused by mans **"casting of God behind his back and despising his word"**. This same situation exists in an individual's life or a nation or a world. The principles apply to all. **[James 4:1], "From whence cometh wars and fightings among you; Come they not hence, even of your lusts that war in your members"?**

This is not what God intended or wants for his creation but that's what he is getting because that's where we are at in our present level of mentality. How did we get here? Who's to blame, can the problems be reversed and solutions, or a solution, be found to remedy the situation? It really doesn't make any difference at this point in time who was, or is to blame for all this erroneous fiasco, we all have to share in that. Some have caused it to happen; others have stood by and were conned into letting it happen when they should have known better, so we all have a share in the blame. A whole scenario of causes and effects are entrenched in our nation and society, and we are certainly witnessing and feeling the effects of the whole mess we have created through our violating of God's Word.

We will have to initially look to the leadership of the nations, those who are responsible, because of their positions as leader's and authorities in responsibility to God and the people for the well being of nations and the people. Regardless of how these leaders became leaders, whether they were elected or just appointed, unto them much has been given; the responsibility of correct, God ordained leadership was and is on their shoulders. **[Luke 12:48], "For unto whom much is given, of him shall much be required: and to whom men have committed much, of him they will ask the more."** We have committed and entrusted much to our "leaders" but have not required much from them, but then we haven't required much from ourselves either. Consequently God has not received much from either the leaders or the followers. If we were to speak of it in the area of rights as we view rights today, God has not received what he, as the creating and loving God, has a right to receive. He does have the right to be loved, worshipped, revered, honored, obeyed, trusted, etc. He has not been allowed his rights: but man in his arrogance demands his own, as if he really has any. Many will disagree with me in my summation of the whole mess, but I couldn't care less: man has one right, *and that is to* *do what God has decreed as right according to His values and standards of thought, thinking, behavior, and conduct.*

We see our whole world wallowing in chaotic misery and death because they refuse to comply with God's will and wishes of righteousness and holiness as revealed, stated, and taught in his Word. William Shakespeare said it quite accurately when he made the statement, **"What fools ye mortals be"**, and the foolishness continues, unabated in all areas and levels of human existence. Unfortunately it has even slithered into the area of the exceptions who through Jesus Christ, have moved from death unto life, from darkness unto light. We have not been as diligent in our **"soberness and vigilance"** as we should have been, and should continue to be. Negligence has its penalties, **[Hosea 4: 6-7].**

There are those among us who though not completely devoured, are nevertheless, experiencing the viciousness of the devil's biting and chewing in his attempts to devour; not even realizing, maybe even enjoying, what is happening to them because of his deception and subtleness. They too, are contaminated with the, *if it feels good, do it,* philosophy of our present day worldly culture. The pleasures of sin for a season **[Hebrews 11: 25]** are still among us, deceiving and destroying. We still experience difficulties in our learning and application of God's word, along the narrow way that leads to life everlasting, but because we have chosen life and blessing through God's provision of the eternal sacrifice of his Son for our sin, our struggles are blessed with his abundant love, mercy, and grace.

It seems we are locked into the "if it feels good, do it society and culture. We have allowed our "leaders" to run amuck with all the various inputs of concepts, ideas, and thoughts about how things should be done, all without the least consideration of God's righteous counsel. With God and his counsel being excommunicated from the public forum for consideration, and the people not demanding that He be reinstated, and His Word encouraged, recognized, and accepted as the **"law of the land"**, how can we expect anything other than the national gridlock of confusion and chaos we are experiencing today in the "land of the free and the home of the brave"? There can never be real freedom when there is not sufficient intelligent and courage to declare, promote, and establish the counsel of God as the standard by which a nation and its people must operate in order to be truly free. And the struggle, with the encroachment of error continues. We have many of "our own countrymen" who will, and are seeing to that.

To be quite frank about the situation, this nation will never be free until we become courageous, brave, and intelligent enough to deal effectively with the problems that have us bogged down, bleeding us dry financially, spiritually, and physically. Today America is experiencing a great famine in the land. Granted we have food and material goods to spare, at least most of us do. But psychologically, mentally, and certainly spiritually in reference to God and his Word, America is starving to death. There is a famine of immense proportions all around us and America is too blind to see it. **[Amos 8: 11], "Behold, the days come, saith the Lord God, that I will send a famine in the land, not a famine of bread, nor a thirst for water, but of hearing the words of the Lord.** The spiritual and moral foundation and roots of our nation are rotting away because of a terrible lack of Godly knowledge needed to displace and correct an abundance of stupidity, hidden beneath a deceptive covering of worldly affluence and material prosperity. Once again the creeping, slithering deception of sin and iniquity continues to wreck and ruin, **[Hosea 4: 6-7]**. Read it again and again, love, study, practice, and meditate on it continually until your spirit is convinced of the need to pursue and attain to the knowledge referred to in order to avert destruction for you and your family.

The tragic deteriorating condition of our nation and her people will continue to be so until we enter into and pursue a total renewing of our minds according to God's divine counsel, **[Romans 12: 1-2]**, for our thinking, thoughts, and ways. Only then will we see a renewing of the thoughts and thinking of the individual and the ways of the nation, **[Isaiah 55: 7-9]**. There are those that would argue that there is nothing wrong with this nation, we are still the greatest nation on earth. I will certainly concur with the latter part of the sentence, but God is the judge of both parts. With all the filth, iniquity, sin, and abomination being splattered across our television daily: we see this as an indication of the level of mentality which has become so characteristic of our national character, our state of the union.

It seems that this once great nation has less to be proud of everyday. How can you claim greatness when the rest of the nations are struggling to maintain positions of 1-3, and we are groveling at an approximate #4 when we should be at 9-10? It is ridiculous to compare our nation as the greatest among the rest when we are far below what we could be, should be, and would be if we had not excommunicated God and his righteous counsel for the building, establishing, sustaining, and maintenance of this nation and people. It still remains the greatest nation on earth, but with the decrepit conditions of the rest of them, that is not saying much. Where is the love for God, his righteousness, for each other, and our nation? **[1Corinthians 13]** gives us a good rundown on this thing called love and our relationship with it as it pertains to both men and nations.

We can be the mightiest of the mighty, the greatest of the great, the strongest of the strong, the most generous of the generous, etc, but without love [charity KJV], and meeting the demands of love, we are nothing but sounding brass and as a tinkling cymbal. We have heard a multitude of sermons where these scriptures are applied to people, but did you ever consider expanding them to include a nation? **[Matthew 22:37-39], "Thou shalt love the Lord thy God with all thy heart, with all thy soul, and with all thy mind, and him only thou shalt serve". This is the first and great commandment, and the second is like unto it, Thou shalt love thy neighbor as thyself".**

We can talk about "love", this first in the list of **"The fruit of the Spirit" [Galatians 5:22],** we can talk about it in conversation, sermons, misuse it, abuse it, write about it, sing about it, etc, etc, but what is it? It would seem to be a phenomenon that is to be learned and can be developed along with the rest of the fruit of the Spirit with the exception of "joy and peace" which take place within our senses and lives as a result of learning and applying the other items of the "fruit".

Let's take the word "affection" as used in **[Colossians 3:2], "Set your affection on things above not on things on the earth."** Your "affection" here is a series of intense feelings and emotions which could also be considered as "love"; intelligently focused on that which has commended itself to intelligent senses and awareness as something of great value and benefit. It might also be unwisely and with outright stupidity focused on some object of desire, **"things on the earth"** that will gradually, deceptively, and eventually destroy you as well as others that are involved with you.

There is a reason we are commanded in **[Proverbs 4: 23], to" Keep thy heart with all diligence; for out of it are the issues of life".** We live in a world that is characterized by the abundance of un-guarded hearts and minds that need renewing unto righteous counsel, God's Word **[Romans 12: 2]. [Genesis**

6: 5], **"And God saw that the wickedness of man was great in the earth and that every imagination of the thoughts of his *heart* was only evil continually**. Thus does [Hosea 4:6] tell us, **"My people are destroyed for lack of knowledge"**. For affect, let's finish the rest of this scripture, **"because thou hast rejected knowledge, I will reject thee that thou shalt be no priest to me: seeing as thou hast forgotten the law, the Word, of thy God, I WILL ALSO FORGET THY CHILDREN"**.

We might put it this way; **"My people, AND THEIR CHILDREN, are destroyed because they choose to remain ignorant of me, my words of life, and my goodness that leads to repentance with life and life more abundantly"**.

In spite of God's guidance and counsel to the contrary, they have chosen to, "set their affection, their desires and delights, their love", on, **[Deuteronomy 30:19] "death and cursing, rather than life and blessing"**. Man's stupidity seems to know no limits nor have any boundaries. **[Romans 1:22] "Professing themselves to be wise, they became fools."** Unfortunately they seem to have also chosen to remain fools. There is a reason why we live in a nation under the burden of stress overload. Once again, it has to do with "lack of knowledge" of God and his righteous counsel and resultant provisions of the application of such counsel. **[Psalms 119:165], "Great peace have they which LOVE thy law [WORD]: and nothing shall offend, or be a stumbling block to, them"**.

[Isaiah 5: 24]; Contrary wise, great stress, turmoil, and strife have **"they that cast God's law behind their backs and despise the word of the Holy One of Israel and are offended at him"**. **[Philippians 4:6-9] Here is Gods promise and remedy for stress release and peace, think on these things: study them, learn them, set your affection on them, delight**

in them, apply them and you won't have occasion for stress. **[James 4:7] "Submit yourselves therefore to God. Resist the devil and he will, take his stress and, flee from you."**

It is futile to attempt to resist the devil without FIRST, submitting yourselves to God. Many have tried this, only to wind up in counseling sessions because they are still being oppressed by the enemy and can't figure out why. A graphic example of this is found in **[Acts 19: 13-18]. "You must be born again", [John 3: 3-7],** placing yourselves under God's loving care and grace. Even then, obedience is required. **[1 Samuel 15: 22], "And Samuel said, Hath the Lord as great delight in burnt offerings and sacrifices, as in obeying the voice of the Lord?** *Behold, to obey is better than sacrifice"*. **[Isaiah 26:3] "Thou wilt keep him in perfect peace,** *whose mind is stayed on thee:* **because he trusteth in thee."**

You may well be saved by God's grace, but you, **[Acts 17:28]** *"live and move and have your being in him"* **by obedience to his word [John 8:29], "doing always those things that please God", and embracing [Hebrews 6:9], "those things that accompany salvation".** If you love, set your affection on, delight in, desire with the whole heart, GOD, then keep his word in obedience with "joyfulness and gladness of heart for the abundance of all things", apply it, be cleansed by it, and continue to grow and benefit within it, all to the glory and honor of God through Jesus Christ our Lord and Saviour. Rest assured, you will benefit from it today, tomorrow, and for eternity. **[John 14:15; Colossians 3:2; Psalms 1:2, 119:2; Deuteronomy 28:47; John 15:3; 3 John:2; 1 Corinthians 10:31; Revelation 19;1.** This thing of love, from God's perspective, deserves a much deeper study than I have given here; but if you are going to benefit from it, you must acquaint yourself with it through your own in-depth **"study, [2 Timothy 2:15], to show yourself approved unto**

God, a workman that needeth not to be ashamed, rightly dividing the word of truth".

The world has its own version of love that is basically sensual, and selfish, pursued for self-satisfaction and self-gratification without regard to the destruction and pain it causes, **[Job 4:20]. [Hebrews 6:9] "But, beloved, we are persuaded better things of you, and things that accompany salvation, of these things we speak, teach and exhort."** May you sense a quickening in your heart because of God's love and respond to him and others in like love, loving as he loves, including loving yourself, **[Matthew 22:39], [John 13:34-35].**

NOTES

IV. WHOSE CHILDREN ARE THEY

A few years back, there was quite a bunch of nonsense from the "authorities" claiming your children belonging to the state. This nonsense flourished for awhile, mostly in state circles, but never seemed to get off the ground. People didn't seem to accept such idiocy, and rightly so. It certainly never set well with me, and because of whatever reason this idea just kind of died off and faded away into the sunset. Or so we thought! The blatancy of that original erroneous idiocy may have lost its momentum, but the devilish concept didn't; it was just camouflaged and resurfaced under a different deceitful strategy. This new strategy came into being and gained ground subtly and simply by the initiating of new insidious laws of deception and stratagem that herded the people into **"corrals of compliance"**.

I have nothing against laws; we would be in a terrible condition without them, however, ill conceived concepts and ideas from mentalities that produce laws that are commensurate with the illness of the concepts and ideas, and imposed on the populace become deadly. These things, as revelations from the hearts of those who produce them, give us a panoramic view of the flawed thinking and resulting erroneous character of these people, [Matthew 12: 34-37]. What is claimed to be for your protection, packaged and presented as such, is become your nemesis. We find these deceptive claims and illusions of population protection are simply methods of attempted establishing state ownership of everything, including your children. We can find the exact scenario that describes this situation with all its players in place and involved in [Ephesians 4: 14], **"That we be no more children, tossed to and fro, and carried about by every wind of doctrine, by the**

sleight of men, and cunning craftiness, whereby they lie in wait to deceive", all for your own good, of course.

Here we have the "children", we of the general populace, the followers; and the others, the leaders, teachers, authorities, and whoever else has been able to muscle themselves into some sort of leadership position as those that **"lie in wait to deceive, those who practice sleight and cunning craftiness"** for the purpose of deception. Satan himself was the first to introduce this graphic deception and it has been going on every since with new methods and evil inventions in the minds and hands of his willing, devoured slaves with their "cunning craftiness". The enormity of this whole scheme from the beginning to the expansion it has developed into in our modern world is beyond the imagination concerning the many things it includes that affect our lives so adversely every day. There is much need for study and prayer with a liberal application of wisdom, knowledge, understanding, intelligence, and common sense, to guide us safely through the maze of our daily activities in this world, **[1 Peter 5: 8]**, **"Be sober, be vigilant; because your adversary the devil, as a roaring lion walketh about as seeking whom he may devour"**.

You and your Christian loved ones, brothers and sisters are his primary target. He conducts himself more as a sneaky snake, slithering quietly about without announcing himself or his intentions, as he looks for opportunities to ambush the unwary soul with his pleasantly presented insidious deceptions. **[2 Corinthians 2: 11]**, A thorough knowledge of this enemy and adversary is essential, **"Lest Satan should get an advantage of us: for we are not,** to be, **ignorant of his devices"**. Once again we are reminded of **[Hosea 4:]**, **"My people are destroyed for lack of knowledge,** including the lack of a good knowledge of Satan and his tactics. With the rejection, neglect, and forgetting of the essential knowledge needed to avert destruction; our lack puts our families in mortal, moral, and eternal danger.

A great deal of this is accomplished under the guise of the "separation of church and state", wherein the imposition of certain laws, rules, regulations, etc. etc. are designed to condition peoples thinking to accept the state's herding of them into their "corrals of compliance" within the fencing made up of these questionable laws, rules, regulations etc. If a person, who opposes this confinement for even sensible reasons, attempts to oppose the "separation of church and state" imposition, they are immediately chastised, ostracized, and demeaned by those who disagree with them and whatever excuse they have for their opposition. This has become especially true concerning the Christian faith and adherence to Biblical principles. This of course would have to occur as the Bible gives a whole different concept of ownership that opposes the state, and of course the state cannot allow that to be the norm of thinking if they are to remain in authority and power.

Let's see if we can get some additional insight to this Biblical concept of ownership. **[Psalms 24:1]** gives us a good place to start our investigation into this question of, "who owns what". We immediately run into problems with this because of the multitudes who reject the Bible and its authority on anything, which of course is the cause of "**wars, wars, and rumors of wars**", **including those that rage within your own members**", **[James 4: 1]**. For an idea, concept, argument, or whatever to be presented, and be positively effective, it must be based on and anchored into a solid proven foundation that promotes the well being of all. Now we have those who immediately claim that the Bible hasn't been proven to be true and that there even is a God. Neither have these skeptics and scoffers proven that the Bible is not true and that there is no God. I prefer to shift the burden of proof on them to waste their own time, efforts and energy on their pointless pursuits of proof unto nothingness. If they think their concept of there being no God is so correct, let them prove it. **[Romans 1:18-20], "For the wrath of God is revealed from heaven against all ungodliness and unrighteousness of men, who hold the truth in unrighteousness: Because that which may be known of God is manifest in them; for God has showed it unto them. For the invisible things of him from the creation of the world are clearly seen, being understood by the things that are made, even his eternal power and Godhead; so that they are without excuse."**

God has, in great and glorious abundance, already proven himself, and there is no way any man could possibly improve on what he has already done and provided as proof of Himself. We have many who, though not highly educated, you don't have to be, that nevertheless have, and exercised the intelligence to except God by faith, with or without proof. Until the faithless, unbelieving, skeptics have proven their claims, I choose to continue practicing what I personally believe, **based on the "goodness of God", [Romans 2:4] the evidence given, seen, and experienced, to stand firmly on the foundation of God's Word.** Certainly God has given us plenty to work with so that **"even the wayfaring fool in his struggle of existence should not err therein", [Isaiah 35: 8].** However, spiritual blindness seems to have no limitations or boundaries resulting in an abundance of "fools" in every level and area of societies and cultures with a great representation of them among our so called "leaders".

Now to the scripture in **[Psalms 24:1], "The earth is the Lord's and the fullness thereof; the world and they that dwell therein."** This should give us a good start in our journey of exploration concerning ownership of "who owns what". In fact it should very well settle the matter, but let's do some additional searching for Biblical nuggets of truth. **[Haggai 2:8],**

"The silver is mine, and the gold is mine, saith the Lord of hosts." There are other scriptures adjacent to this one that are worthy of consideration and study in connection to this one, but this one gives direct reference to ownership, so it is the only one considered in this discussion. We cannot exclude the other elements of great value such as diamonds, pearls, rubies, etc. etc, but must include them all in this ownership declaration. It would be foolish to exclude them simply because they were not listed, as the use of silver and gold here certainly make reference to all things that are of value regardless of the extent of that value. **[Psalms 89:11], "The heavens are thine, the earth also is thine: as for the earth and the fullness thereof, thou hast founded them." [Job 41:11], "Who hath prevented me that I should repay him? Whatsoever is under the whole heaven is mine." [1 Corinthians 10: 26-28]; "For the earth is the Lord's, and the fullness thereof: Vs. 28, for the earth is the Lord's, and the fullness thereof."** We have been given, for reinforcement and emphasis, this particular scripture twice in these verses. These are all in addition to the many creation scriptures in Genesis.

We, and our children are a part of that fullness, regardless of what the secular state and its proponents and sympathizers claim. I realize that there are multitudes that will disagree with the Bible perspective on this subject. They have full control over what choices they choose to believe, but they do not have the slightest control over the facts that God himself has established and set in place for eternity, nor do they alter the facts by their disbelief. If, in the final culmination of all things, it is found that they were right, what have they gained in their point of view, what have they proved that was worth the expenditure of their life, seeking their proof. Without exception, we would all be lost. If, however, there were even just the slightest possibility of the Bible's inerrancy in this matter, then we who believe have won all things now and forever, and they who have chosen to wallow in their disbelief have lost all things for all eternity.

What a shame, but that for a simple swallowing of their destructive pride, repentance of sin, a turning away from their evil ways, and believing in the gospel of truth unto obedience, they could have alleviated an eternity of horror, misery, and agony; and enjoyed the presence and pleasures of God for ever. I am absolutely astounded at the stupidity of supposedly intelligent beings that continue to prove themselves otherwise who chose to remain in the death and cursing position rather than following God's direction and command to choose life and blessing for themselves and their "seed", their children, **[Deuteronomy 30:19-20]**, their seed and children, their posterity, being referred to as **"their blossom"** in **[Isaiah 5: 24]**.

[Psalms 16:11], "Thou wilt show me the path of life: in thy presence is fullness of joy; at thy right hand there are pleasures for evermore." For just a few moments of time in repenting and accepting Jesus Christ in all his fullness, whether it be with intelligence or out of desperation to escape the plagues and delusions of this world, they could have had all the rewards and benefits provided and available to the Christian believers, not only in this world, but for the same eternity that they, because of their pride, arrogance, and ignorance, will otherwise suffer through. What a terrible, terrible tragedy that they committed themselves to a devil's hell and sentenced their children along with them because they **[Deuteronomy 30:19], "chose death and cursing rather than God's provision through Jesus Christ as Saviour, of life and blessing"; because [Hosea 4:6] they despised, rejected, neglected, and subsequently forgot the law, word, of God with all it's life giving knowledge.** Well has Shakespeare said **"What fools ye mortals be"**.

Through the questionable educational system that has devolved downward to it's present inept, sorry condition by whatever erroneous decrees have been made as to its control, our children are being, day by day further alienated from parents, God, and his principles of righteousness, purity and the morality that is essential to the development of a nation and society wherein is found that which God intended for us to have and enjoy. In this we must include the Biblical Christian character of our children. It is only on the establishment of this character and its further development on into adulthood that will guarantee a successful nation. Only on execution of **[2 Chronicles 7: 14]**, **"If my people, which are called be my name, shall humble themselves, and pray, and seek my face, and turn from their wicked ways; then will I hear from heaven and will forgive their sin, and will heal their land"**, can America or any nation be restored, redeemed, or re-created in this age. God has made some very sensible requirements in order to gets the benefits and results we so desperately need in our nation and lives. The same principle applies and works for the individual life as well as the land of which the individual is an integral part.

This pursuit of happiness that is mentioned in our constitution has become just that, a pursuit, without any hope of attainment because of the excommunication of God and the despising of His Word. This happiness, which includes peace and joy is only found within the boundaries and substance of God's Word, counsel, and direction, and only alluded to in clever deception elsewhere, such as the constitution. In the present degraded condition of our nation, the pursuit has become a hopeless struggle, and much of what was in the past attained to is rapidly being lost due to the "separation of church, primarily the Christian experience, and state" being twisted and degraded into a "separation of God and people" by our judges and their blind followers. On 9/7/07, when watching a news channel, they were telling of the increase in teenage suicides and wondering what the reason for it was.

The state has shut them off from God wherein is found the hope of mankind. Thus in playing the part of the thief in **[John 10: 10]**, and being his willing associates, they have stolen, killed, and destroyed the hope that is only available through Biblical teachings and adherence. Certainly these young people can take a look around them and see there is no hope of a fulfilled, soul prospering life under state laws, rules, regulations, and a perverted constitution. Their only hope is in Jesus Christ; and the state, with the willing assistance of some of our "own countrymen", has forbidden that in the public arena and is making it increasingly difficult in the private sector.

Thank God for the exceptions who have held their ground and refused to yield to the secular state's unreasonable judgments and demands and increasing idiocy. The training, conditioning, and rearing of our children cannot be left up to anti-God, anti-Bible influences, the input of the world system. It is an unfortunate situation that in today's post-modern world after several generations of non-Bible compliance by the national and civil authorities, that many parents are not raising their children as God intended they should, but are in fact supporting the state position in its **"sleight and cunning craftiness", its deceptive practices.** A Biblical principle and perspective on this is found in **[Deuteronomy 4]**, the principles that were given to the Israelites in particular but apply to all nations down through the ages in there appropriate application. In **verses 9-10 of this chapter, we find specific directions as to teaching children about the wonders, glory, and power of God, also in chapter 6: 6-7, there is continued direction and commands to the teaching of the children; it continues in [11:19], "And ye shall teach them to your children, speaking of them when thou sittest [in thine house], and when thou walkest by the way, when thou liest down, and when thou**

risest up," IN THINE HOUSE, AT HOME, AROUND THE KITCHEN TABLE, WHEREVER, but at home. Fathers, mothers, what are you doing in teaching your "seed" about this great God; Jehovah is his name?

Are you leaving it all up to Mom, the Sunday school teacher and the Pastor? Mom, how about you? Are you taking over where Dad has dropped the ball, or are you united and committed together as God's team in the raising and nurturing of your "seed", or do you even care, or are you even aware of **God's counsel of righteousness? [Proverbs 4: 23], "Keep thy heart with all diligence; for out of it are the issues of life."** Parents; if you are not obedient to this: how do you ever expect to train your children in it? **If you don't train yourself in how to keep your own heart with all diligence, how are you going to teach your children in this; or even provide an example of doing this?**

If you fail in this, you may well find yourselves caring and raising your own grandchildren instead of their parents who have no clue in how to raise them because you never taught them how nor provided an example for them to follow. We see this in overwhelming abundance in America today. Do you even understand the significance and value of being successful in this child rearing situation? If you fail in this, be assured the idiot child psychologist's who wrote all manner of books on child rearing that prompted and contributed to your failure are not going to step in and bail you out of your dilemma. They made big bucks off of their books which was their motive for writing them, but never had the success of your child rearing efforts or the wellbeing of your children in mind, nor could they care less.

It is a sad situation when our national leaders are not qualified to, and so do not encourage the people, all the people to adhere to the Biblical Christian principles on which this nation was founded, that formed the foundation in which it was once anchored. What happened among our leadership and the constituents that have served, not to build our country, but to bring about its demise? **[Hosea 4: 6; Isaiah 5: 13], "My people are destroyed for lack of knowledge: because thou hast rejected knowledge, I will also reject thee, that thou shalt be no priest to me: seeing thou hast forgotten the law of thy God, I will also forget thy children."** Our leaders have used the separation of church and state deception as a miserable excuse to **cast away the law of the Lord and despise the "word of the Holy One of Israel" [Isaiah 5: 24],** bringing our nation to the shameful condition and state is in today. They have enjoyed much encouragement from others of **"our own countrymen",** in the ACLU, People for the American Way, etc, etc, who do not in reality represent a true America, and whoever else has, and is contributing to the demise and degradation of our nation through the rejection and neglecting of God's principles of life and life more abundantly.

These are commensurate with those evil kings and leaders of whom it is spoken in the Old Testament who **"made all Israel to sin."** There are approximately twenty-three references in 1st and 2nd KINGS of evil kings; leaders, of Israel "who made all Israel to sin". We certainly have their counterparts with us today, and still of "our own countrymen". There were those "few exceptions" that led Israel in the ways of God and his laws, but there were a few, very few. I will leave it up to the readers to make their own comparisons between the ancient and the recent unto the present. History does indeed, repeat itself, and well it will, for the evil nature of man that so affects it continues.

God is still God and his agenda is still in force, sin is still sin and the wages of sin is still death. God's judgment is set in respect to sin and he will not change his mind or his agenda concerning it. There were practices of abomination under the rebellion of Israel in relation to the treatment and sacrifice of their own children in worship of these false gods that would make you sick if you were to witness it today. But they became conditioned to it over a period of time and were blinded to the filth and degradation that they practiced and wallowed in. It became business as usual, "just the way life is".

We, in like manner, have become conditioned to the atrocious abomination of abortion, the sacrifice of millions of unborn babies to the gods of immorality, convenience, and the irresponsibility that so many of "our own countrymen" have come to worship. But it is legal and thus, "politically correct". Aren't we Americans proud of ourselves for our great accomplishment of discovering and initiating the "evil invention" of "political correctness" that has made room for all manner of abomination and transgression to be established in our society? Now we don't have to be responsible for decency, morality, and just doing what is right by God's standards and values that God declares we must to gain favor with him and be accepted with him, **[Acts 10:35]**, **"Then Peter opened his mouth, and said, Of a truth I perceive that God is no respecter of persons: But in every nation he that feareth him, AND WORKETH RIGHTEOUSNESS,** *is accepted with him"*. We have attempted an end run around God by our cleverness of being legal and "political correct". Indeed, **"What fools ye mortals be"?**

It is sickening to realize that we are having, and raising children up in this squalor of immorality and filth that is becoming so characteristic of our beloved America. It is no wonder the old Indian stands on the bluff overlooking what once was a beautiful, clean river and now sees the garbage that it is polluted with, and tears run down his cheeks. We must remember, however, the river was not responsible for its own pollution. The pollution belongs with the ones who have a mind to pollute. Once again the gods of irresponsibility and profit are worshiped with a mind that, in itself is suffering from self imposed mental, psychological, and spiritual pollution that is so characteristic of a degraded people and nation.

And this is what the non-Christian, secular humanistic, atheistic, the usurpers of dominion authority, portion of America is teaching our children, in the classrooms you are paying for. If it feels good, do it, everything is relative, what's wrong to you maybe alright for me; it depends on how I feel about it, after all, I have my rights and; right or wrong, moral or immoral, I may change the way I feel about it tomorrow so my conduct will change accordingly regardless of how you feel about it or how it adversely affects you. After all, I've got my rights. And America wallows in this incompetent mental garbage. Is it any wonder we are suffering such shame and disgrace as a nation and people? And the modern day Christians have stood by, wringing their hands in despair, whining and complaining, and done nothing to prevent it; being conned into believing that if they just attended church and Sunday school and paid their tithes and offerings, everything would be alright. In the meantime behind the scenes, the God opposing elements of our nation have taken control of the controlling governing elements, such as making and imposing rules, regulations, laws, etc to exercise such control.

There is no part of this garbage that coincides with or is allowed by God's absolutes, which is why God's word is ridiculed, scorned, and despised by the world we live in. This world can't stand the truth; it condemns and convicts the transgressor and makes them to uncomfortable to tolerate such conviction of truth. [Job 5: 6-7], **"Although affliction cometh not forth of the dust, neither doth trouble spring out of the ground: Yet man is born unto trouble as the sparks fly upward"**. [Isaiah 50: 11], **"Behold, all ye that kindle a fire;**

that compass yourselves about with sparks: walk in the light of your fire, and in the sparks that ye have kindled. This ye shall have at my hand; ye shall lie down in sorrow"**. Tolerance is only tolerated by them when they want you to be tolerant of their intolerable conduct and activities. Diversity is only recognized when they wish for the Christian to diversify in their direction and favor their erroneous positions, in support of their production of "evil fruit", **[Matthew 7:17-18]**.

I am no longer concerned about offending those who produce, promote, tolerate, approve, condone, or protect this character destroying trash, that under our illustrious constitution they have been given the right to contaminate our society with, even to the production and distribution of the mind and soul destroying filth of pornography. The longer our young people are subjected to this world and its anti-Bible concepts, the more of them will be destroyed for lack of the essential knowledge, **[Hosea 4:6]**, of God's life giving truth; and the longer we allow it to continue, the longer they will be subjected to it; and the longer the destruction will continue. And business as usual continues also. I am not surprised at the increase in teen suicides; their erroneous pseudo authority controlled culture has robbed them of a meaningful future and a hope for it. Jesus Christ is still the answer and solution to this disgraceful dilemma, as He is to all the rest of them.

Whether we like it or not Mr. and Mrs. America, we are at war for the minds, hearts, lives, and souls of our children as well as ourselves. If we neglect to get our own minds in a renewal mode, we cannot possibly help and assist our children. God, and the input of his righteous counsel, for the hope of man's survival and life, must become our top priority. For the hope and life of your children, God must be your top priority. If he is not your top priority, it is very doubtful he will be theirs, and all is lost.

It is deplorable to see our nation sacrificing the lives of its young people in the mid-east in an attempt to "win the hearts and minds" of those people to democracy and we of the church are so lacking in winning the hearts and minds of our fellow Americans to the Lord. There is no comparison of importance between the two. But there, as here, if there is no interest or cooperation from the other side, not much will be accomplished. There is room for a lot of thought and discussion concerning this. Jesus has eternity to offer; democracy without God hasn't got squat.

Take a good long look at America with her democracy and the magnitude of problems we have, just because God has been kicked out and his word thrown out after him. This is the heritage America without God is leaving to her children. Thank God for the exceptions! I would like to issue the challenge of becoming one of God's exceptions to the multitudes. It is going to take a whole lot more than just being a citizen of "the land of the free and the home of the brave, a land that is not free because of her sin and iniquities, with a populace that neither has the wisdom, intelligence or the courage to effect is freedom under God's divine directives.

The people are the nation: as the people go, so goes the nation. Israel lost their identity as a nation of prominence several times because **they cast the word of God behind their backs and despised the word of the Holy One of Israel.** Is America so arrogant and ignorant as to believe they can escape God's judgment for their like abominations, sin, and desecrations of his word? Do we think that just because God has blessed us so abundantly in the past, that he will make an exception of us in the administration of his judgment for the iniquity, filth, and spiritual rebellion that has penetrated into the heart and soul of our beloved America? Who can be held to account for this but our leaders, from the top; presidents, supreme court judges, right on through the ranks of leaders to the parents and role models of our young people. Anyone that has influence in the lives of others has to share in the blame. Consequently, none of us are completely innocent. Those at the helm of our nation must, however, assume the greater responsibility, and bear the greatest burden of guilt. They have completely failed to lead the nation based on Biblical presented principles and directions God has given us for the construction of a spiritually prosperous nation where our children can grow up and develop into good trees bearing good fruit, having eternal purpose pleasing to God. It is impossible to separate the national politics from God's truth, absolutes, and counsel, and expect that nation to prosper.

Instead they are in a nation where known sexual predators are allowed to run loose and pornographers are allowed to assist and encourage them in their evil endeavors. Something is terribly wrong with this picture. With the exception of the few in **[Matthew 7:14], "Because strait is the gate, and narrow is the way, which leadeth unto life, and FEW there be that find it"**, the whole nation is in slavery to sin and the "iniquity that is found in thee", [Ezekiel 28: 15]. The land of the free and the home of the brave is being held in question. What a horrible legacy of the damnation of destruction our leaders have passed down to their younger generations of acquaintances and families. Recently the term "culture of corruption" has appeared on our national scene. I couldn't help but wonder who it might have been that coined that phrase, but it certainly fits the day and age we have degraded into.

There is not much friendship in all this conglomeration of confusion. Friends, if they indeed be friends, just do not destroy each other, nor set the stage for them to destroy themselves. Where are the leaders who will learn and promote the **"Fruit of the Spirit"**, **[Galatians 5: 22-23]** among the people; administering justice when it is needed against who and whatever is set against this Godliness and righteousness, and would destroy it if they could, and at the present time are doing a pretty fair job of it. **"But God"!**

Opposition against these destroyers seems to be weak to non-existent. Indeed they are encouraged by the supreme court and lesser court judgments against God, his word, and his program of deliverance, redemption and reconciliation through Jesus Christ. Any other "religion" doesn't get the static and opposition that Christianity does in what has been termed "a Christian nation". *The reason for this may well be that no other "religion" presents the truth that sets men free, nor also brings the uncomfortable conviction of sin to a man's heart and soul that the truth of God's Word does, so in an attempt to maintain some sort of deceptive comfort it becomes necessary to remove this "Christian religion" that provides for man's salvation,* **[Romans 1: 18-32], verse 32, "Who knowing the judgment of God, that they which commit such things are worthy of death, not only do the same, but have pleasure in them that do them."** It really makes you wonder who or what is running this country, and **the thief continues "to walk about as a roaring lion seeking whom he may devour", [1 Peter 5: 8]**, and is doing a pretty thorough job of it.

[Proverbs 22:6], "Train up a child in the way he should go: and when he is old, he will not depart from it." This scripture is very interesting in that it seems to give this person considerable leeway between being a child, and getting old. It certainly is best when a person in their younger years is taught, learns, and exercises wisdom, knowledge, understanding, and intelligence in their lifestyle, and as a result is delivered from the pain of a "prodigal son experience. Unfortunately the majority of young people experience this with a minority of them ever **"coming to themselves" and going home, [Luke 15: 11-24], verse 17, repenting and believing the gospel, [Mark 1: 15]** Thus the majority remain in the worlds pig pen of existence for the remainder of their days and die there, never knowing about the God that loves them and sacrificed His Son for them because the state forbids such knowledge in the schools and very few of them are getting it at home. Unfortunately these delivering qualities, even when known about, are hard to learn and apply with all the distractions of the world around us. They are attained to normally a little at a time through the years with our trial and error experiences as we live, make mistakes and we hope, learn, correct our mistakes and move on to our later years. This slow, often by trial and error process seems to be tragically characteristic of mankind.

For some reason humanity keeps making the same dumb mistakes over and over again. We can observe others do some dumb, ignorant things, see them pay for it, have historical accounts and records of them, and then go do the same stupid thing ourselves, and do it over and over again. Going needlessly into debt seems to be one of the main culprits. The use of discretion in this for some reason or another has eluded the majority with great regularity. Been there, done that, don't like it, won't go back, can't afford it anyway, spiritually, psychologically, or financially. Who needs it? There are other areas of serious entrapment to the unwary, unknowledgeable, foolish, and otherwise just plain stupid.

The Book of Proverbs is full of Godly wisdom to guide the young and unwary, and remind the older in the course that God has set for us to travel and develop our lives. The truth that prevents and delivers man from sin and iniquity is not limited by any means to Proverbs, but is found from cover to cover within God's Word. I have heard it said, "that, you can't legislate righteousness". I don't know from what ignorance of thought this came from except to say it has to be a worldly ridiculous bit of wit in another feeble attempt to discredit God's legislation of righteousness found cover to cover in his Word which righteousness gives us life , peace, and joy among many other Biblical taught and presented benefits.

I have found the Bible a source of legislation of righteousness throughout, from cover to cover; the one and only source of Godly legislation that is available to men and women, both young and old, with specifics for each and general directions, admonitions, and commandments for all. **[Psalms 119:165] "Great peace have they that love thy law, and nothing shall offend nor be a stumbling block to them."** Learn to love God's word young person, older person, learn it and learn to love it and enjoy it together for the mutual well being, enrichment, and profit of all, including above all, the glory, honor, and pleasure of God, **"for the earth is the Lord's, and the fullness thereof; the world and they that dwell therein." [Matthew 19:14] "Suffer the little children, and forbid them not, to come unto me: for of such is the kingdom of heaven."** Young people, little children, all; you have a special place in the heart of God, dwell there in love and obedience and be nourished in Godliness unto a **"perfect man, unto the measure of the stature of the fullness of Christ", [Ephesians 4:13]. This is your heritage provided by God himself. Don't allow others to rob you of it including those of "your own countrymen", which in some, too many cases, may be those of your own household, [Matthew 10: 34-36].**

Remember, that regardless of how young you may be, the years pass quickly, and all to soon the majority of you will reach adulthood and become parents. Parents, prepare your young people for this. Remember how quickly it came around to you. Due to the busy-ness of our post-modern era, it will come around sooner for them, or so it will seem. **[Proverbs 22: 6], "Train up a child in the way he should go: and when he is old, he will not depart from it."** As the parent, it is your responsibility under God's divine direction and counsel, to determine the way your child should go, not the states. They have proven year after year, generation after generation, they do not have the wisdom, knowledge, understanding, intelligence, and common sense to do it.

*To neglect to do this has got to be the worst form of child abuse ever devised, whether intentionally or unintentionally, as the results of rebellion and transgression against God and his Christ are not a simple paltry twenty year or life sentence; **they are eternal** under the worst possible conditions.*

NOTES

V. BIBLE ONLY

In the interest of establishing and maintaining a value of purpose, direction, and destiny, temporal as well as eternal, only the Holy Bible, the Word of God, will be considered in these writings. The KJV will be the version used with an occasional use of another version at times. Unfortunately Biblical value is a value that relatively few, considering the masses, put any stock in, thus it is not often considered as worthy of thought or pursuit and is uncomfortable with its truth and convictions. The reason for this is that it does have considerable restrictions concerning sinful conduct, and seeing as man is so involved and given to such conduct he naturally despises any correction for his erroneous behavior.

Nevertheless, the Bible is the only source of complete truth and absolutes as to the overall well being of man including his spiritual prosperity the ages have provided. This "Word" originated outside of the extremely limited intelligence and abilities of man who have turned their backs on God and formed their own "religions" under the direction and coercion of the evil they have chosen for themselves and their posterity with its death and cursing, **[Deuteronomy 28; 30:19-20]**. This is a situation where it is hoped that the apples will fall far from the trees, however, such is not often the case.

The Bible is the Constitution of the ages and creation, given by God for the direction and course of humanity. This is to be the means of execution of the divine dominion granted by God to this one whom He created in His image and likeness for this purpose. This Constitution of Creation is, always has been, and always will be, the Supreme Law of the Land, presiding over all the lesser constitutions devised and formed by man in his attempt to establish, without submission to, and direction from God; some sort of order within his society, nation, or country.

All of these lesser constitutions must by necessity be subservient to this divine "Constitution", **"given by inspiration of God, which is profitable for doctrine, for reproof, for correction, for instruction in righteousness: That the man,** or nation, **of God may be perfect, thoroughly furnished unto all good works, and prosper therein, [2 Timothy 3: 16-17]; the good works that God has before ordained that man should walk therein"**, **[Ephesians 2: 8-10]**.

The permanency of this Bible, this **"Constitution of the Ages"** that reveals the content of the heart and mind of God for the benefit of His creation is shown in **[Matthew 24:35; Mark 13:31;** and **Luke 21:33]**. Contained in the passing away of the earth is the inclusion of all the lesser constitutions devised and conjured up by man. All these lesser constitutions, regardless of how noble or important they were esteemed to be, compared to the Eternal Constitution given by God, are and will to be found worthless and of no profit. Though respected, honored, and esteemed for a time, they too, **"like the life of a man, and being a product of man, is even a vapour, which appeareth for a little time and then vanisheth away"**, **[James 4:14]**. *"Tis only one life, twill soon be past, and only what's done for Christ will last".*

When the winds of time, opposition, and false doctrine are put to rest and cease to blow, and the dust of disobedience, destruction, and iniquity, has settled to the ground, standing unscathed and victorious, as strong as noble as ever will be that Heavenly Constitution, the Bible, the Living Word of God. Gathered around that eternal structure will be the multitudes who loved it, revered it, studied it, lived by its divine promises and eternal principles, and enjoyed its living presence. These will be rejoicing in this One of **[John 1:1-14]** who set them free to **"worship and serve Him with joyfulness and gladness of heart for the abundance of all things"**, **[Deuteronomy 28:47]**. Unto the remainder of humanity, the unrighteous and unholy who "chose death and cursing, [Deuteronomy 30:19, instead of life and blessing; He that is unjust let him be unjust still: and he that is filthy, let him be filthy still", [Revelation 22:11]. [Matthew 6: 2], "Verily I say unto you, they have their reward".

This Christian experience may be considered as a religion and has certainly qualified as such, but the term "religion" is so loosely and commonly used in our world today that it lacks the specifics needed to identify any particular religion whenever one is being considered. This is true especially of the Christian "religion". It is often used with the intent of elevating the lesser to the position of the greater in an attempt to give the lesser some sort of credibility by forcing a blending together in an overall inclusion where they are all equal. This has never been, nor will it ever be acceptable to God and his people. Therefore if the term is used in these writings it will generally, and specifically, be considered as referring to the Christian Religion for the purpose of its specific identity and exclusion of all contrary religions and beliefs, as there is a definite difference. Within the doctrines and teachings of the Christian "religion" there is life and life more abundantly for the adherent to its gospel message, while exterior to this there is only an existence of sorts to be endured, temporal and eternal.

The difference lies in the fact that the Christian belief structure, the Christian Religion, is the only one that starts with mans beginning, and if obeyed, provides for all his well being, benefits and rewards, both temporal and eternal for all men everywhere. It requires nothing of him but that which is conducive to common sense and intelligence that is beneficial to his relationship with God and others, providing specifically for the enriching of these relationships in their normal God ordained development. Because of this, the Christian faith, religion, persuasion, belief, etc, can and will be the only one considered and recognized as absolute in its truth and contributions to fulfillment of its promise of life and life more abundantly. All that is external and contrary to this God established truth is deception and falsehood resulting in confusion, chaos, and calamity, bringing death and destruction.

This is one of God's great and precious promises and cannot be cancelled, altered, annulled, nor diminished, making it an exercise of futility to even attempt to include or consider anything else, for all else is of lesser value to no value at all, being in fact, detrimental to any further advancement and development in righteousness. It is a promise to all who will accept God's provision of salvation, redemption, and reconciliation through Jesus Christ, Gods once for all, forever sacrifice for all sins for all men for all time. It is his immutable Word. Live by obedience to it or die by neglecting, rejecting and, or despising it. Argue against it and disagree with it if you will; you will lose, agree with it, live by it, and you will live; both today, tomorrow, and forever.

There are multitudes of people who are willing to settle for lives so shallow that they barely qualify as an existence. Then there are those who want depth, substance, fulfillment, and purpose, who truly receive of their desires for a deeper more fulfilling, meaningful relationship with their Heavenly Father, Almighty God, for these things are to be found only in God and it is there that they find them, **[Matthew 5: 6], "Blessed are they which do hunger and thirst after righteousness: for they shall be filled".** This relationship is also God's own desire and will for each and every one of us. Only an existence is to be found in this world with all its pointless pursuits with very little, and ultimately nothing, to show for the efforts expended by those who settle for this shallow existence with its pointless pursuits. It is good to enjoy the fruits of our labors here, but there is more to life than to just spend our allotted time here and then die with nothing lasting beyond this life to show for it.

God has given us the opportunity to build here for that which extends beyond **"life that is as a vapor that appears for a little time, and then vanisheth away", [James 4:14].**

I have been blessed to enjoy much of what God has provided in his creation. I do wish I had learned to appreciate it more much earlier in my life. I'm certain it would have enabled me to enjoy it even more, but quite often age reveals things that younger eyes never saw. In my later years of a deeper appreciation and gratitude for God's provision, I have developed a growing disgust for the world man has created for himself within the beautiful creation that God provided for him, as well as for the people that insist on continuing this demise. It grieves me somewhat to realize that I was once a contributor to the wretchedness that continues to plague mankind and makes me very thankful for God's provision of repentance, forgiveness and deliverance through Jesus Christ our Lord and Saviour. Not only has man messed in his own nest, he has made a mess out of what God provided for him to begin with.

If man had the backbone to follow God's "to dress it and keep it" instructions to Adam in the Garden of Eden, we would be living in a much nicer world. In spite of man's transgressions there is still quite a bit of this creation that remains very beautiful, but although it still retains some beauty, man's idiotic influence has nearly destroyed its "niceness". Modern man, like ancient Adam, has disobeyed God's word and reduced his world to a survival like existence worldwide. Many are starving for various reasons that can be directly connected to selfish, corrupt leadership, while those who have the resources to do so spend their time harvesting whatever fun and games, pleasure and worldly delights they can while they are here while rarely, if ever, having any serious thought about the eternity that awaits them. Thank God for the exceptions.

It seems that man attempts to design his world to prioritize these amenities because of his desire and lust for them and because many of them are quite profitable. However, many of these endeavors are more destructive than they are profitable; for once the monetary benefits are gone, the destruction caused in the meantime lingers on and has eternal consequences for those adversely affected by the loss of eternal values that have been neglected during the interim. The pursuit of these things leave very little if any time for the **"diligent seeking of God"** who is the ultimate provider of **"all things that pertain to life and Godliness [2 Peter 1:3]"**, so man continues to indulge himself in these "amenities" that hasten his demise.

These indulgencies are no challenge to their somewhat demented mentalities to advance and develop themselves beyond their dementia to the point where they begin to shed their dead skin of existence and take on the signs of the life that God created them to have and enjoy. This would of course involve some rather intensive study and because **"much study is a weariness to the flesh [hard work]",[Ecclesiastes 12:12]** and no fun, man shies away from such challenges and continues to devote himself in pursuit of that with which he can entertain and destroy himself. Thus does man continue on the path of least resistance, after all, it is easier to drift with the flow of demise with the satisfaction of the fleshly, uncontrolled desires and lusts, than it is to swim against the current of fashion, normality, and tradition to reach the goal of "righteousness, peace and holiness, **"without which no man shall see the Lord." [Hebrews 12:14]**.

Time wasted on foolishness is foolishness indeed, and as time is generally what our life on earth consists of, and it is not guaranteed, let us say that a life consumed with foolishness is a life wasted on the most gross foolishness, without God, peace, joy, happiness, purpose, fulfillment, etc. There's fun and pleasure of sin, yes, but only for a season **[Hebrews 11:25]**, and a short one at that with more heartbreak, turmoil, and misery, than one can afford. That is the result of sinful indulgencies, and you can rest assured, sin carries its own retribution. Time, or life, must be invested in something at least equivalent to its own value, and your life is of immense value whether you realize it or not, or it becomes time and life wasted. If you do not place the value on your life that God places on it you may well **"choose death and cursing rather than life and blessing, [Deuteronomy 30:19]**. The world with its glitter and glamour and false promises of better things to come will deceive you into doing this, but the choice will be yours. After all, God has given us all a choice; **"therefore choose life and blessing that both you and your seed [children, descendents] shall live"**.

As to time and life invested; invest your life in that which guarantees a good return on that investment to yourself and others by taking God's investment advice and choosing life and blessing. God is pleased with your choice of obedience. You will continue to experience the joy and peace of God's blessing on obedience, and others will be blessed because of your blessings that come with the "territory", your dwelling in the presence of God. **[Psalms 36:7][John 8:29].** If a person desires greatness, that person, by necessity, must learn to be a servant of all. Esteem and recognition may be granted by man for various purposes, but true greatness can only be granted by God and that on the basis of his values and standards. Tops on God's list of requirements is what we might term as "servanthood" **[Matthew 23:11]. "But he that is greatest among you shall be your servant"**. We serve God, and man, by obedience, **"doing always those things that are pleasing to God"**. Jesus left us this example in **[John 8:29]; "and he that sent me is always with me, the Father hath not left me alone; for I do always those things that please him"**. Jesus himself came to

serve; not to be served, [Matthew 20: 28]. What a glorious challenge and example he has given us.

Time spent in service to God and others is the best investment of time and life and has the greatest "guaranteed" returns. God will see to that, he has promised; **[Matthew 6:33] but, "seek ye first the kingdom of God, and his righteousness; and all these things shall be added unto you".** The paydays are God's concern and we can always depend on him to be more than fair and just. **[2 Peter 3:9]; "The Lord is not slack concerning his promise, as some men count slackness; but is long suffering to us-ward, not willing that any should perish, but that all should come to repentance".**

We must learn to find our rewards in the satisfaction of the exercising "greater love", the example of Jesus, by the laying down our lives of self service, to live in his service, forsaking and repenting of any selfishness and self centeredness, and living our lives in obedience to God's desires for the benefit of our friends and others, even those that despitefully use us and oppose themselves. This must all be tempered with the application wisdom, knowledge, and understanding, lest you suffer from violation of **[Matthew 7:6], "Give not that which is holy unto the dogs, neither cast your pearls before the swine, lest they trample them under their feet, and turn again and rend you."** Discretion must be used in the application of some scriptures as to whether they will be applied when dealing with unruly members of the Christian family or dealing with non-Christian people who do not acknowledge Biblical principles of behavior and conduct. Unfortunately we do have some church members among us who have some shady tendencies of behavior that surface from time to time. If we rely on our own concepts that have not been submitted to the teachings of Godly counsel, we all can transgress in these areas. It is a good idea to keep repentance close at hand as it is often needed.

God's word not only teaches his wisdom, knowledge, and understanding, but also implies the utmost in intelligence and common sense. This must be done lest we **"give place to the devil and allow him an advantage over us by being ignorant of his devices, and methods", [Ephesians 4:27], [2Corinthians 2:11].** It is that lack of knowledge, ignorance, of the devils devices, knowledge that God wants us to possess, that contributes much to the destruction mentioned in **[Hosea 4: 6]**.

[John 3: 17]: "For God sent not his son into the world to condemn [or destroy] the world, but that the world through him might be saved". The mission of Jesus was to save the world, and to this end he lived according to his Father's desires and will to accomplish that which was set before him. **[John 4:34], "Jesus said unto them, my meat is to do the will of him that sent me and to finish his work".** Jesus was the means to the Father's end of implementing the plan of salvation, redemption, and reconciliation of the world and all men through the eradication of sin.

Jesus made this available and possible through his teachings, his gospel, his life, his ministry and finally his death on the cross as a ransom for many **[Matthew 20:28].** Jesus certainly laid down his life by living it to and including the cross experience; **[Luke 22:42] not according to his will, but that his Fathers will might be done.** This is how we lay down our lives, by denying and destroying our selfish desires in order to accomplish, as Jesus did, the Fathers will. **[Matthew 10:39], "He that findeth his life,** in selfishness, **shall lose it: and he that loseth [lay down] his life,** of selfishness, **[by living]** it in service, **for my sake shall find it".**

Living your life for "Jesus sake" is finding your life and life more abundantly. Learning, knowing, and living Biblical principles is the answer to living life, for these things, when obeyed, guarantee life with it's many God ordained rewards for such obedience. To live them is the epitome, the height and glory, of "servanthood". To learn and live these principles is to manifest **"the excellency that is in them", [Job 4:6],** so we do not die without this excellency lived within us, and the wisdom to exercise it for the glory, honour, and pleasure of God. This is "finding your, true, life", not some fake existence that people attempt to pass off as life without Jesus in control through his teachings and reaffirming the principles that have always been in and a part of God's heart.

These "principles" of, love, kindness, goodness, righteousness, holiness, purity, Godliness, etc, the "Fruit of the Spirit", [Galatians 5:22-23; Eph. 5:9-17]; there are others such as patience and forgiveness along with many others that are available to the person, who with intelligence, will ascertain the value of these provisions and avail themselves of them. This will give you something extremely profitable and productive to do for the rest of your life. To make a list of them is a good thing to try to do, and a magnificent learning exercise to be sure. To memorize them is of limited value, though to recite them may be impressive to some.

It is the studying, learning, and living of them that is of a necessity. It is the life of **"doing always those things that please him", [John 8:29], the revering of God and working of righteousness that makes us acceptable to him, [Acts 10:35], following the command to, repent ye and believe the gospel, [Mark 1: 15] and receiving of his forgiveness and "amazing grace".[Ephesians. 2:8] "For by grace are ye saved through faith; and that not of yourselves: it is the gift of God."** It is on this foundation of saving faith and grace that we build **with works of righteousness [Acts 10: 35], that are acceptable to God,** *Jesus Christ himself, being the chief corner* *stone and substance of this foundation, the living manifestation of the fullness of God.*

[1Cor.3: 9-11] Vs. 10: "But let every man take heed how he buildeth thereupon," [this foundation.], the rock. [Matthew 7:24]. "Therefore whosoever heareth these words of mine, and doeth them, I will liken him unto a wise man, which built his house upon a rock: and the rain descended, and the floods came, and the winds blew, and beat upon that house; and it fell not: for it was founded upon a [the] rock." This "rock" is the same rock of [Matthew 16:18] upon which Jesus is building "his church", the rock of revelation truth that Jesus is who God has revealed and declared him to be. This is the church against which the storms and gates of hell cannot and shall not prevail. This is the "house", the church, the life, the family, the nation, the whatever; "that except the Lord build the house, they labor in vain that build it", [Psalms 127: 1].

Many are the "houses" that have been built in vain because the directions and blueprints of God's counsel have been despised and rejected in the construction process, **and the "rock", the [Isaiah 28:16] "sure foundation" has been despised and cast aside in favor of the reality of the stupidity of man as shown in verse 15**, preceding verse 16. It is amazing that with all the historical and present evidence as to man's constant failure in his endeavors, he continues to refuse God's counsel. He still insists, in his pride and arrogance, on building it himself, whatever it is and regardless of the cost, yet without regard to God and his counsel. Indeed, **"What fools ye mortals be"**.

Thus does the stupidity and idiocy of man continue to be manifested in the degradation of, not only themselves as individuals, but their cultures and societies. **Thank God for the**

exceptions who wholly follow the Lord their God, [Deuteronomy 1:36], [Joshua 14:8-9; 14:14]. There are magnificent benefits in "wholly following the Lord God of Israel," this [Acts 10:35] reverencing of God and working of righteousness.

For those who might consider the use of words such as stupid, stupidity, ignorance, idiocy, idiot, imbecile etc. to be a bit harsh and offensive, let us consider the facts and then be honest about your own summation of the use thereof. For and examination of the use, lets turn to, you guessed it, the Bible, for the input needed for study, looking beyond man's "intelligence" and making our decisions. **[Deuteronomy 30:19-20],** Here is one of those, "one size fits all" principles of Gods word given to all men everywhere that has nothing to do with the controversy that is carried on over law versus grace.

It is, however, a law that when the correct choice is made with God's counsel and direction it will introduce his "amazing grace". It states, **verse 19, "I call heaven and earth to record this day against you, that I have set before you life and death, blessing and cursing: therefore choose life that both thou and thy seed may live".** We will ultimately be known by the choices we make. We will either prosper with wisdom at God's hand, or suffer by victimizing ourselves with stupidity, depending on these choices. They reveal our mentalities and determine our conversation, conduct, and behavioral patterns. The content and abundance of our heart will reveal us to the world around us. God already knows.

Considering what is at stake here, with us being born into the death and cursing mode of sin, and an opportunity to be delivered from that dungeon of existence unto a life and blessing state of being; think about this for a minute. If you were in prison on a life sentence for something and you have an opportunity to correct it and be released with a full pardon, and you made a choice to refuse the opportunity to do so with the resultant freedom and blessings yet to be revealed, would you be wise and intelligent or stupid and ignorant? The choices you make, in your thinking and thoughts, positive or negative, right or wrong, good or bad, evil or righteous, etc, is the direction your speech, your conduct, your behavior, will take. These choices will be made out of the content of your heart according to your developed mentality, your attitude, up to that point in your life or existence, whichever is apparent by your present and manifested lifestyle.

We are faced with a conglomeration of "rights", constitutional, civil, personal, guaranteed, etc, etc. They all come under two definitive terms, positive versus negative. Positive rights establish and promote the good and well being of all. They are based on wisdom, knowledge, understanding, and intelligence, honoring God, his principles and counsel, his WORD. Negative rights are all based on a "if it feels good, do it" concept that is buried in the arbitrary, fickle, irresponsible, selfish, moment by moment ever changing human emotions and feelings, resulting **in the wages of sin, [Romans 6:23], which still remains "death".** We might also refer to these rights as being good versus evil, or even intelligent versus stupid.

Our national foundation was formed on a God given system of principles, standards, and values, by our founding Fathers, which if adhered to would have advanced and promoted our nation and her people to a state of greatness which now, in her present condition, seems totally out of reach unless **[2 Chronicles 7: 14]** is initiated, and soon. This system was and is based on God given absolutes and can never be dependent on vacillating human emotions, which is as Jacob said of his son, Reuben in **[Genesis 49:4], "thou art as unstable as water"**.

You must understand that democracy without God is a failing system, as unstable as water. It may well be the best there is for a form of human government, but without God at the helm it will, has, and is, destroying itself, as have all human governments who have rejected God's counsel and direction and forged ahead in disobedience and rebellion against Him. **[Isaiah 5: 20], "Woe unto them that call evil good, and good evil; that put darkness for light, and light for darkness; that put bitter for sweet, and sweet for bitter",** whether they be individuals or governments.

With a few exceptions, Americans have sunk and are continuing to sink to lower levels of abomination and degradation through the continuing exercising of their negative "if it feels good, do it" rights, totally disregarding the system of righteousness that Jesus Christ appropriated for them for their present and eternal well being. Any way you look at it, whether you like it or not, stupidity and idiocy are rampant and rapidly becoming characteristic of America and her people. **Once again, and I stress this point; thank God for the exceptions.** There are, at least, a few. They are not to be found, however, in the ranks of the ACLU and like organizations or individuals sympathetic to such anti-God, anti-Christ positions.

[Isaiah 5:20-24], "Woe unto them that call evil good, and good evil; that put darkness for light, and light for darkness; that put bitter for sweet and sweet for bitter. Vs. 21 Woe unto them that are wise in their own eyes, and prudent in their own sight. Vs.22 Woe unto them that are mighty to drink wine, and men of strength to mingle strong drink: Vs 23, which justify the wicked for reward, and take away the righteousness of the righteous from him [with the separation of church and state, or to be more precise, the separation of God and people]. Vs. 24, Therefore as the fire devoureth the stubble, and the flame consumeth the chaff, so shall their root be as rottenness, and their blossom shall

go up as dust: **BECAUSE they have cast away the law [WORD] of the Lord of hosts, and despised the word of the Holy One of Israel"**.

Making judgments and decisions against the Ten Commandments is just a start. If this nation, after enjoying God's abundance of blessings since its inception, is to any degree cognizant of God and his majestic, divine relationship to his creation and they refuse to bow in obedience to his counsel and direction, it has to be the most gross manifestation of stupidity this world has ever been witness to. And we are all to blame for allowing it to happen. Either by rejecting or neglecting our calling, responsibilities, privileges, and duties to God and each other, we are all responsible, each to some degree, for America's plight.

It saddens my heart to see the demoralized condition of this nation that we are leaving as an inheritance to our young people. We owe them an apology for allowing this great nation to get to the condition it is in and then expecting them to fix it after indoctrinating them with the same mentality that has brought us to our present state of being. Even so Lord Jesus, come quickly. If we are to build the **[Matthew 16:18]** church upon the rock of the revealed truth of God concerning who we are, the church against which the gates of hell shall not prevail, **we must see its emergence and affect on our society soon.** Obviously, it must contain and manifest some wonderful things that many of the churches up to this present day have not. There are a few but not all, that seem to exhibit, possibly with some of the **[John 17]** unity, harmony, verses 11, 21-23 oneness in Jesus. Indeed, we need to learn to set together in heavenly places with you Lord, being of one mind and one accord. **Thank you Father, for your love, patience, and forgiveness which are some other things we need to learn which would**

certainly help in that condition of being one with each other and you.

God is opposed to two things, sin and the mentality that is commensurate with it that accepts, practices, and promotes it. The sin may be described as abomination, iniquity, unrighteousness, ungodliness, evil, rebellion, conformity to this world, etc. etc. The commensurate mentality, which is best identified with it may be described as foolish, stupid, ignorant, nonsense, arrogant, and others wherein man has demonstrated his natural sin conditioned abilities and proficiency. This is all referred to and addressed in **[Romans 12:1-2], "I beseech you therefore, referring to earlier and other scriptures, brethren, by the mercies of God, that ye present your bodies a living sacrifice, holy, acceptable unto God, which is YOUR REASONABLE service. And be not conformed to this world: but be ye transformed by the renewing of your mind, that ye may prove what is that good, and acceptable, and perfect will of God".**

You, your, ye; it sounds like it is us and we who are being addressed here as to the need of a mind overhaul. Let me assure you that professing Christianity or becoming a Christian does not automatically cause this to take place in our lives. Repentance of sin and accepting Jesus Christ as your personal Lord, Saviour, and King certainly places you in the family of God but it also introduces you into God's classroom. This is where the learning and gaining of wisdom, knowledge, understanding, intelligence, and Biblical spiritual experience is taught, and hopefully learned, acquired, remembered, and practiced, thus establishing the Biblical standard of excellence for all, being manifested in each individual.

There is a multitude of things that will appear periodically under these, foundational requirements, which you will learn throughout your life, mostly and preferably, through much study.

Wise is the man who learns from the lumps on the other fellow's head.

Bad experiences and their results are best learned from observance rather than by personal involvement with unpleasant and painful participation. However, history has proven over and over again that man does not learn well from others or his own experiences, whether they are personal or national. Our nation is experiencing things today that have historically destroyed other nations and still we insist on pursuing those same stupid, rebellious, destructive things in opposition to God's will and desires. We have not learned, as a nation or individuals, from the lumps and bumps on our own or the other fellow's head. It will never happen to me or us, seems to be the prevailing attitude, and when it does happen we are quick to blame someone else, even and preferably God.

Political parties blame each other for our national problems, never having the courage and intelligence to admit that their own political parties and efforts in excommunicating God and his righteous counsel from our nation and her people have been their own contributions to our national dilemmas. This Jehovah God and his righteous counsel can and will be only found in the Christian religion, faith, persuasion, experience, call it what you will, but it is the building material of the foundation of our America. You cannot find this abundance of wisdom and power for direction and purpose in any other religion and definitely in human built organizations. **[Psalms 127: 1], "Except the Lord build the house, they labor in vain that build it".** I am not opposed to these people of other religions; they can only live what they have been taught. But on examination of their end result based on their practices, you might think they would be searching elsewhere for an alternate place to spend their eternity. **[John 14:6], "Jesus saith unto him, I am the way, the truth, and the life: no man [regardless of his religion] cometh to the Father, but by me"**. It takes more than taking on the title of Christian, or claiming to be one to actually be one **[Acts 10:34-35], "Of a truth I perceive that God is no respecter of persons: BUT in every nation he that feareth [reverences] him and worketh righteousness is accepted with him"**.

Anyone can claim to be something but, **"a tree is known by his fruit"; [Matthew 12:33; Luke 6:44]**. I realize that we are saved by grace through faith in Jesus Christ, and not by works, but once this has taken place it seems that the **"working, or works, of righteousness that God hath before ordained that we should walk in them", [Ephesians 2:10],** has a definite impact on our relationship with God and on our being **"accepted with him"[Acts 10: 35]**. It ought to inspire us to explore this area of the **"working of righteousness"** and see if we can develop an understanding of what it consists of, considering its importance, and be involved in this as an expression of gratitude for this gift of "amazing grace".

[1Peter 4:17], "For the time is come that judgment must begin at the house of God: and if it first begin at us, what shall be the end of them that obey not the gospel of God"? Judgment beginning at the house of God; maybe it would be a good idea if we Christians from time to time would **[2 Corinthians 13:5], "Examine yourselves, whether ye be in the faith; prove your own selves. Know ye not your own selves, how that Jesus Christ is in you, except ye be reprobates"?**

It would be good to know how we personally "stack up" in the possession and use of these fruits and gifts of the Holy Spirit. Good, honest, self-examinations would certainly help in this process with continued study, especially in the areas where we come up short. To be "born again, saved" by God's grace, cleansed by the blood of Jesus, is a most wonderful experience. We should all, simply out of gratitude for this gift of "life and life more abundantly" pursue lifestyles of willing obedience that are **[Colossians 3: 28], "well pleasing to the Lord"**. After all, this is only our **"reasonable service" [Romans 12:1] of loving God with all our heart, with all our mind, and with all our strength, [Matthew 22:37, living and moving and having our being in him, [Acts 17: 28].**

[Ecclesiastes 12: 11-12], "The words of the wise are as goads and as nails fastened by the masters of assemblies, which are given from one shepherd, [2 Timothy 3: 15-17]. And further, by these, my son, be admonished: of making many books there is no end; and much study is a weariness of the flesh". We find in **[1 Corinthians 3: 9-11]** the apostle Paul fastening some goads, and nails, those things commensurate with God's principles and absolutes which provide stability and strength, into the assembling of the foundation of truth on which all men may build lives, careers, families, churches, and nations and whatever else is essential to successful progress and development. **[Psalms 127:1], "Except the Lord build the house, they labour in vain that build it: except the Lord keep the city, the watchman waketh but in vain".** [1 Corinthians 3: 9-11], **"For we are laborers together with God: ye are God's husbandry, ye are God's building. According to the grace of God which is given unto me, as a wise master builder, I have laid the foundation, and another buildeth thereon. But let every man take heed how he buildeth thereupon. For other foundation can no man lay than that is laid, which is Jesus Christ".**

Though "much study is a weariness of the flesh" we are admonished in **[2 Timothy 2: 15-16], "Study to show thyself** approved [unto God], a workman that needeth not to be ashamed, rightly dividing the word of truth. But shun profane and vain babblings: for they will increase unto more ungodliness"**. It would seem that among this "making of many books there is no end", that there are some that need to be shunned and rejected as being nothing but "profane and vain babblings" which, because of their distracting and destructive nature and teachings, "will increase onto more ungodliness".

We must understand that though these books may make the authors and publishers much money, which is their sole purpose regardless of their "vain and profane babblings", they are not worth the paper they are written on and definitely not worth the time taken out of your life to read them. Your life is valuable, your time is valuable; don't waste it on time consuming **"things wherein there is no profit", "that add nothing of value to you", [Jeremiah 16:19], which tends to the increase of more ungodliness.**

This life consuming junk is of overwhelming abundance in our world today with more of it coming off the presses by the hour. **[Proverbs 4: 23], "Keep thy heart with all diligence; for out of it, the diligently kept heart, are the issues of life".** However, we find that the soul that is affected by the heart that is not diligently kept in God's counsel, that issues forth death, shall surely die, **[Ezekiel 18: 4], "Behold, all souls are mine; as the soul of the father, so** also **the soul of the son is mine: the soul that sinneth, it shall die".**

Be extremely careful and selective, using wisdom and discretion in what you expose your mind to even if it be just reading for entertainment. If that which tends toward degradation of moral stability and character is appealing to you, you've placed value in the wrong areas and must, by necessity, embrace and diligently apply **[Romans 12: 1-2], "I beseech you therefore brethren, by the mercies of God, that ye** present your bodies a living sacrifice, holy, acceptable unto God which is your reasonable service. And be not conformed to this world, but be ye transformed by the renewing of your mind, that ye may prove what is that good, and acceptable, and perfect will of God". "And ye shall know the truth and the truth shall make you free", [John 8: 32].

NOTES

VI. ONE GOSPEL, TWO MESSAGES

The Gospel message, the Good News concerning Jesus Christ, the kingdom of God come down to man, for the purpose of bringing salvation to a lost and condemned humanity without hope, without purpose, without reason for being, without GOD! This is the first and only message, the call to repentance, so that this lost and hopeless being might know the **"riches, goodness, forbearance, and, longsuffering of God", [Romans 2:4], that leads men to repentance, salvation, and redemption.**

This forbearance and longsuffering is being graciously administered today to those who are ignorant of the abundant "goodness" of God. It awaits those who exercise sound reason and **[Isaiah 64: 7] "stir up themselves in obedience to take hold of God"** in making the right choice that God commanded them to make in **[Deuteronomy 30:19-20]: "I call heaven and earth to record this day against you, life and death, blessing and cursing: therefore choose life, that both thou and thy seed may live: That thou mayest love the Lord thy God, and that thou mayest obey his voice, and that thou mayest cleave unto him: for HE IS THY LIFE AND THE LENGTH OF THY DAYS; that thou mayest dwell in the [area and calling of life wherein the Lord thy God shall choose to place you"].** [Ephesians 4: 11-16] gives us some examples of these callings which are at God's discretion.

Originally given to the Hebrews for their specific purposes, there are commandments, principles and directions of Godly counsel and advice stated here that have remained applicable down through the ages and apply to all mankind. All are commanded and counseled to, **"choose life and blessing so that both they and their seed shall live"**. This is a universal calling and appointment to all people everywhere. Whether or not they heed the call and keep their appointment is up to the individual. There may be a specific geographical location were God by his providence shall place you for his specific purpose. For the Israelites it was **"the land which the Lord sware unto thy fathers, to Abraham, to Isaac, and to Jacob, to give them"**. Your geographical location may well be where you live today, tomorrow maybe somewhere else of God's choosing, but regardless of where it is, there is a spiritual "area" wherein God has placed us all.

That spiritual area and calling is the same for all, an area of **[Isaiah 64:7], "stirring up thyself to take hold of God, to love the Lord thy God with the whole being", [Deuteronomy 6:5-6], and to [Deuteronomy 28: 47], "serve the Lord thy God with [an attitude] of joyfulness, and with gladness of heart, for the abundance of all things"**. This all is contained in a love desire to **[John 8:29], "do always those things that please him", learning and doing [Hebrews 6:9] "the better things that accompany salvation", all under the simple, understandable concept of "OBEDIENCE"**.

There is no way that I, or anyone, could possibly relate to anyone else the extent of the wonders and glories of heaven that await the child of God, the born again, believing, new creation saint. **[1 Corinthians 2:9-10], "But as it is written, Eye hath not seen nor ear heard, neither have entered into the heart of man, the things which God hath prepared for them that love him. But God hath revealed them unto us by his Spirit: for the Spirit searcheth out all things, yea the deep things of God"**. The Bible reveals a multitude of wonderful things about our heavenly home that awaits the truly repentant sinner; the **"new creature in Christ saved by the grace of God", [2 Corinthians 5: 17[**, but we fail to grasp the magnitude of it, nor can we, and there is still much left to be revealed and learned. **[Ephesians 2: 7], "That in [and throughout] the ages to come, he might show the "exceeding riches of his grace in his kindness toward us through Christ Jesus"**.

The Spirit of God does a rather magnificent job in presenting and revealing much of that which is to come to us. It is the receiving of that information, processing it understanding and doing it, that seems to present the problem. **[Proverbs 4:7-8], "Wisdom is the principal thing; therefore get wisdom; and with all thy getting get understanding. Exalt her, and she shall promote thee: she shall bring thee honour, *when thou dost embrace her*"**.

There are set before us some conditions for developing and attaining to a successful and meaningful life in Christ. God himself in his wisdom, knowledge, and understanding, has determined and established these conditions. Man has done the same, however without the intelligence and other Godly requirements needed for such a noble undertaking. Try as he might, his concept of success is infinitely lower and different than God's. Consequently his requirements, reasons and ideas for attainment are also equally as low and destined to failure. **[Isaiah 55:8-9], "For my thought are not your thoughts, neither are your ways my ways, saith the Lord. For as the heavens are higher than the earth, so are my ways higher than your ways, and my thoughts than your thoughts"**.

Man's highest, without any thought, intention, or effort, of revering and honoring God, though seemingly useful for a time, in the final hour will prove useless, worthless, and will without a doubt, contribute to his digressive, final downfall, and ultimate destruction.

If man would exercise himself in getting a vision of what is valuable by God's standards that is contributive to the over-all well being and enriching of his personal self as well as others who he will influence, we would no doubt witness a change in the conduct in our societies and cultures throughout the world. This will take considerable meditation, study, and concentration of thought directed toward the truths and absolutes contained within the precepts, counsel, and principles of God's word. It would also involve the submission and dedication to the execution of these life giving truths and principles, thus to God, **[James 4-7]**, himself through Christ Jesus, our Saviour and Lord. This is all contained in, and a result of, **[Romans 12: 1-2], "the renewing of the mind"**. Man is, however, hampered in this area by a multitude of self imposed obstacles, the basis of which are two characteristics of humanity, *selfishness and pride*, which stem from such things as a total lack of wisdom, understanding and knowledge of Biblical matters, spiritual and practical.

[Proverbs 16:18], "Pride goeth before destruction and a haughty spirit before a fall". Thus is man destroyed, being ignorant, **[Hosea 4:6, lack of the knowledge]** of Godly requirements and instead, overloaded with the temporal things of this world which may give him much pleasure, periodically and momentarily, but rob him of his life, preventing him from having a wholesome relationship with the God who created him. This relationship is precisely why God gave his Son Jesus to redeem us from sin and reconcile us back to himself, blessing him and being blessed by him for eternity, to enjoy his abundance forever.

Though there is a lot yet to learn about this heavenly home and eternity; this is what awaits those **who love and serve him with joyfulness and gladness of heart for the abundance of all things, [Deuteronomy 28:46]**. This is not the reason for doing these things, but the results of doing them with the right attitude, for this is what God has in store for those who do these things out of thanksgiving and gratitude for such abundance and eternal provisions. **"For God so loved the world, that he gave his only begotten Son, that whosoever believeth on him should not perish but have everlasting life", [John 3:16]**. This scripture is probably one of the best known and most memorized in the Bible, and is not only the basis, but a very thorough, though brief, outline of the entire Bible gospel message. Everything that is meaningful pertaining to our lives and our relationship with God is to be found somewhere in the depths of this one scripture. It is up to us to exercise the determination and diligence of intense study to find it.

What is contained in it, and the greatness of God's love for his creation, what is the completeness of what we received when God gave us his Son, what are the implications of believing on Jesus, what is the glorious fulfilling of this "everlasting life": that is the gift of God? Many questions arise in the inquisitive, searching mind. We may wonder, what are the causes that result in mans rebellion against God that bring about his destruction? Why does he indulge in such idiocy unto his own demise and destruction? **[Hosea 4: 6-7]** gives us some insight into the answer: an extreme lack of knowledge, knowledge that needed to be past down from generation to generation, knowledge that would avert such destruction, knowledge that only comes from diligently studying God's Word.

As for the answers and solutions needed to solve our multitude of self imposed problems; **[Matthew 7:7-8], "Ask, and it shall be given you; seek, and ye shall find; knock, and it shall be opened unto you: For everyone that asketh receiveth; and he that seeketh findeth; and to him that knocketh it shall be opened".** Therefore, [2 Timothy 2:15], **"Study, diligently, to show thyself approved unto God, a workman that needeth not to be ashamed, rightly dividing the word of truth".** [John 14:26],**"But the Comforter, which is the Holy Ghost, whom the Father will send in my name, he shall teach you all things and bring all things to your remembrance, whatsoever things I have said unto you".** [Psalms 119: 104], [Proverbs 4: 5, 7; 16: 16]

For the beginning and proper introduction to this gospel message, this teaching and our remembrance of it, we would have to go to **[Luke 2:9-11], "And, lo, the angel of the Lord came upon them, and the glory of the Lord shone round about them: and they were sore afraid. And the angel said unto them, Fear not: for I bring you** *good tidings of great joy, which shall be to ALL people.* **For unto you is born this day in the city of David a Saviour, which is Christ the Lord".** We must include verse 14 here as it gives us the essence of God's intent toward his creation: **"Glory to God in the highest, and on earth PEACE, GOOD WILL toward men".**

This becomes extremely important in our post-modern world of today when we are witnessing so much violence in the name of religion. We see no peace or good will toward men expressed in this, but only blind followers and blind leaders, caught up in a senseless chaos of selfishness, greed, hatred, animosity, murder mayhem, etc, etc. This is all far removed from and totally opposed to the gospel of peace mentioned in the previously quoted scriptures. It graphically presents an area where the "leaders and rulers; those operating under and in accordance with the divine authority and power of God are to step in and exercise that authority and correct the situation using whatever measures and means necessary to accomplish the task, **[Romans 13: 3-5]**. Had they, according to God's design and intentions, assumed and wisely performed their responsibilities and duties previously, they would have prevented much of this mountain of chaotic problems. **[Ecclesiastes 8: 11], "Because sentence against an evil work is not executed speedily, therefore the hearts of the sons of men are fully set in them to do evil".**

Whatever or whoever allows, condones and promotes this opposition to God's design and will for his creation must be, by wisdom and intelligence, discarded immediately for it all constitutes sin with its resultant wages of death and destruction, which curses come upon the entire nation guilty of such transgressions. Unfortunately, it may become necessary, for the advancement of God's good and righteousness, to also discard the vessel that obstinately insists on possessing dishonor and evil, thus continuing the pollution and contamination of our culture, society, and nation; **[1 Thessalonians 4: 4; 2 Timothy 2: 21],** even if it be in the subtle form of a contrary religion.

For this reason I hesitate to use the term "religion" in reference to the Christian experience unless the word "Christian" is used in conjunction with it as to identification of the "religion" being referred to. It would be an offense to God to allow the lumping of Christianity in with the contrary religions of the world, all of which, because of their very nature and teachings, are opposed to Christianity and thus to **"Jesus, the author and finisher of the Christian faith", [Hebrews 12:2].** This Bible, Gods Word, with its Christian religion and Godly principles established as the foundation of America, must be guarded and kept and promoted as such, or America will perish as all other nations before her that have rejected this Word of God with its righteous content. We see multitudes of nations around the world that have lost the essence of life within them because of the imposition of contrary religions and now survive only as an existence described in **[Isaiah 5: 24], "Therefore as the fire devoureth the stubble, and the flame consumeth the chaff, so their root shall be as rottenness, and their blossom shall go up as dust: because they have cast away the law of the Lord of hosts, and despised the word of the Holy One of Israel". [John 14: 6], "Jesus saith unto him, I am the way, the truth, and the life: no man cometh to the Father, but by me".**

Unfortunately, we are seeing some *advanced signs and results* of that very rejection, and neglect taking place today in great grand and noble America, the "land of the free and the home of the brave". This somewhat modern description of

America is rapidly fading away into the fog of chaotic deception because America too, is guilty of **[Isaiah 5: 4]** because of forsaking her Biblical established roots. This makes this message of **[Luke 2:9-11, and 14]** extremely important to our nation and world today along with additional supportive scriptures concerning the gospel message found throughout the Bible. The importance of the message, to be affective, must break through the ignorance and foolishness of humanity to take root and grow. The availability of fertile ground where this seed of gospel truth can take root and develop into the fruit of salvation of souls seems to be quite limited. Nevertheless, God will not be set aside by the abominations and sinful agendas of man. *His gospel of peace and good will toward man through Jesus Christ, Saviour, Lord, and soon coming King is still available, for whosoever will, may come.*

Forget about attempting to prove God's existence; God has already proven that quite grand and gloriously. It is just that the blind and rebellious refuse to accept it, **[Romans 1: 18-22], "For the wrath of God is revealed from heaven against all ungodliness and unrighteousness of men, who hold, suppress or bind, the truth in unrighteousness, Because that which may be known of God is manifest in them; for God hath showed it to them. For the invisible things of him from the creation of the world are clearly seen, being understood by the things that are made, even his eternal power and Godhead; so that** *they are without excuse: Because that when they knew God, they glorified him not as God, neither were thankful; but became vain in their imaginations, and their foolish heart was darkened. Professing themselves to be wise, they became fools".*

The scorners and skeptics who profess themselves to be wise, will never accept anything as proof of the existence of God. Their foolish pride will never allow it. They have become loud and arrogant enough, as blind leaders, to deceive and blind a world into following their "pernicious ways" *by reason of whom the way of truth shall be evil spoken of".* [2 Peter 2:2], "And many shall follow their "pernicious" ways; [Hebrews 11:6], "But without faith it is impossible to please him [God]: for he that cometh to God must believe that he is, and that he is a rewarder of them that DILIGENTLY seek him".** The rewards and benefits of God are reserved for the faithful that **serve him with joyfulness and gladness of heart for the abundance of all things, [Deuteronomy 28:47].** There is an attitude of being willing, with joyfulness and gladness in serving God that is of extreme necessity and importance, being well pleasing to the Lord. Good, pleasant, proper, God pleasing, attitudes of love for God are often difficult to retain and maintain once they have been developed; if developed. **[1 Peter 5: 8], "Be sober, be vigilant; because your adversary the devil, as a roaring lion, walketh about seeking whom he may devour.** Remember, you are his target and he, with his destructive intent, is also and very definitely, *no respecter of persons.*

It does take considerable thought and determination coupled with self-discipline, which is also from time to time, quite elusive, to attain and maintain this zeal for further development unto Christian maturity. Concerning Godly principles and correct attitudes, there are three "elusives", *diligence, determination and self-discipline,* which if not attained to, established, and practiced for perfecting purposes, causes man considerable problems. There are a multitude of other things, that man in his rejection and rebellion, by the general appearance of things, has employed in his efforts to destroy himself, which by that same appearance shows that he is quite successful in his determined attempts at self destruction. This is not what God had, nor has in mind for his creation.

Once again, we are reminded in **[Romans 6:23], "The wages of sin is still death.** This has not changed, nor has it been canceled over the ages, **but the gift of God, as presented by the good news of the gospel of God, is and will continue to be, eternal life and life more abundantly."**

In this we find, one gospel of good news with its message of life and life more abundantly with its blessings, and one message pertaining to death and cursing, which of course is not good news, but a definite sincere warning of the wrath to come for the unbelieving, rebellious, sinner. We find in this Gospel of God a message of hope and assurance based on the promises of God for those who according to God's counsel, choose life and blessing, repenting and believing the gospel, for themselves and their "seed". There is another message to the unrepentant sinner who scorns and rejects God's word and counsel and the results of such rebellion and disobedience. One gospel, two messages, and the choice remains, yours. **[Proverbs 1:7], "The fear of the Lord is the beginning of wisdom and knowledge: but fools continue to despise wisdom and instruction".** And the choice still remains, yours.

NOTES

NOTES

VII. PEACE

It is amazing how some words take on an aura about them that radiates a certain sense of their meaning when they are spoken or written. Although it does help considerably to understand the language being spoken! "Peace" is definitely one of those words. Just to think of peace in writing or talking about it brings a sense of calmness to the spirit, soul, and mind, if you are concerned about it at all, where otherwise there may be a sense of turmoil and stress with the age old American pastime of worry.

The only thing I could ever see about worry was that it had a strong tendency to keep people from finding solutions to the very things they were worried about. They would rather clutter their minds with worry about things than exercising the self controls to construct the Biblically oriented, God pleasing, soul prospering, lifestyles that prevented the majority of the things they worried about from ever materializing. Maybe worry is the only excitement some people experience in their lives, so they worry for entertainment.

I've seen some segments of soap operas, and I couldn't help but wonder; are people actually stupid enough to live like that? It does seem like there are many who do with lives of continual turmoil, animosity, and strife? In remembering way back when I was a lad when there was a radio "soap opera" called "Young Doctor Malone", a forerunner of today's television soaps. I had an aunt and a grandmother who faithfully listened to it. I remember as they were doing some ironing one day, getting into a pretty heated argument over some different points of view concerning certain fictitious characters in the program and thinking to myself; what a waste of time this was when the mind could be used to think about good productive things. But there wasn't much for excitement in those days, just a lot of hard work, worry, and radio soaps.

I don't remember the word "stress" being a commonly used word describing a condition people experienced when I was much younger. I'm sure people experienced it; they just didn't know what to call it yet, so we never heard of it, but being well versed and experienced in "worry", they settled for that until the new modern version of "stress" surfaced which sounded much more impressive. **So now people worry about their stress.** In the past several years it has surfaced quite regularly and seems to be a way of life with some folks. Maybe there are more things to cause such a condition now than there used to be or possibly people have just gotten farther away from that, or He, which would tend to alleviate such "stress". *Worry and stress* seem to be as conjoined twins, inseparable and destructive. They do their evil work in the lives of multitudes the world over and are not excluded from the Christian segment of society, but are alive, well and continually used; well worn, but not as yet, worn out.

[Proverbs 3] gives some sound direction for avoiding these two twins, but unless people have been taught these specifics they may simply read them as a spiritual exercise rather than adopt them as an absolute truth of Bible directed deliverance. Consequently they never learn to incorporate them into their lifestyle, thus being able to benefit from them. Many of the Bible directed solutions for deliverance from stress and worry are as practical as they are spiritual.

Peace however, is seldom found in the non-Christian majority of society where the "Prince of Peace" is scorned and rejected, and his word despised. Even among Christians where the Word of God is the instruction manual of life and living; simply neglecting of the Word in study and practice will have a devastating effect on peace and tranquility. It doesn't automatically take place simply because a person becomes a Christian. Even in accepting this word and reading it; the neglecting of it in daily living, the doing of it, has destroyed many lives, marriages, and careers. This neglecting, along with the rejecting of the "Word of God", and consequently God himself, is the process that destroys peoples and nations. Just reading the word for a spiritual exercise is like just hearing it; it is fruitless unless it is applied. **[Psalms 119: 104], "Get wisdom, get understanding: forget it not; neither decline from the words of my mouth"**. **[John 15:3], "Now ye are clean through the [applied] word that I have spoken unto you"**.

Over an extended period of time, *neglecting*, no application of, *the Word* will have the same affect as rejecting it in the beginning. Our nation is experiencing the affects of both rejecting and neglecting of God and his Word. God and his Word are inextricably joined with his church. Since our noble leaders have ignorantly, constitutionally separated God's church from the state, they also separated God and his counsel from the state and, inevitably, from the people. Once again we see **[Isaiah 5: 24], "Therefore as the fire devoureth the stubble, and the flame consumeth the chaff, so their root shall be as rottenness, and their blossom shall go up as dust: because they have cast away the law of the Lord of hosts, and despised the word of the Holy One of Israel"**. And once again I am reminded of our old friend Shakespeare's immortal words, **"What fools ye mortals be"**. Why is humanity so stupid as to consistently and in some cases, violently, reject the simple principles of obedience to God's Word, which he has so lovingly and generously provided for our own benefit and profit?

Unfortunately we do not seem to have the leadership, collectively or individually, with the wisdom, courage and backbone to correct this "stressful" situation; so we contend with it from day to day, as an element of "business as usual", not as best we could with God's direction and counsel, but as best as we have become accustomed to without God's direction and counsel. We are not, even as Christians, accustomed to spend time in prayer that is accompanied with faith, obedience, and trust in God for the needed solutions, nor is there the deep meditative study of God's Word that should be the norm and love of professing Christians. As a result, a destructive deterioration has set in, affecting nearly all areas of life with few exceptions. Thank God for those few exceptions that do help stabilize the remainder and infuse "peace" throughout.

Peace: use your dictionaries to study and get a good solid sense of the various applications of the meaning of "peace", and then pursue it. There seems to be different levels of peace that are to be attained to in our study, exploration, and discovery of this Bible taught principle and treasure. Let's begin our search for this peace in **[Philippians 4:5-9], "Let your moderation be known unto all men. The Lord is at hand. Be careful for nothing;** don't get stressed out [worry] over worldly situations and conditions, **but in every thing by prayer and supplication with thanksgiving let your requests be made known unto God. And the PEACE OF GOD, which passeth ALL understanding, shall keep your hearts and minds through Christ Jesus. Finally, brethren, whatsoever things are true, whatsoever things are honest, whatsoever things are just, whatsoever things are pure, whatsoever things are lovely, whatsoever things are of good report; if there be any virtue, and if there be any praise, think on these things".**

It is interesting to note here that the idea of what is legal versus what is illegal is not considered, but the higher and more noble idea is called to mind of what is morally right versus what is morally wrong, or immoral, according to God's standards and values, **[Isaiah 5:20].** Man has deemed many things legal that are immoral and wrong, and made illegal some things which are not only morally right but have been ordained and commanded by God himself. Thus has man in his ignorance and stupidity attempted to usurp God's authority and establish his own in opposition to God. Consequently, our "land of the free and the home of the brave" is be hopelessly trapped in conditions of idiocy, chaos, and confusion with destruction hot on our trail. However, **[2 Chronicles 7:14] remains a viable solution to our multiplied dilemmas if we ever get desperate enough to initiate it.** It just might take some advanced desperation to do it as sufficient intelligence to get the job done seems to be totally absent from the American scene.

There was a Bible character named "Lucifer" who tried this "usurpation of God's authority" and got thrown out of heaven for his efforts, **[Ezekiel 28:15]**. Those who attempt this same folly today don't have to worry about being thrown out of heaven, they just won't get there. There is a place reserved for them and their father the devil "Lucifer", **[Isaiah 5: 14], "Therefore hell hath enlarged herself, and opened her mouth without measure: and their glory, and their multitude, and their pomp, and he that rejoiceth, shall descend into it"**.

[Philippians 4: 6-9], verse 9, "Those "things", which ye have both learned, and received, and heard, and seen in me, do: and the God of PEACE shall be with you". No particular description of peace is given here, just simple instructions and exhortation to pursue it. **[1 Peter 3:10-11] "For he that will love life, and see good days, let him refrain his tongue from evil, and his lips that they speak no guile: let him eschew evil, and do good; let him SEEK PEACE AND ENSUE IT"**.

ENSUE: Here is a word that is not commonly used that is connected with **"peace"**. I had to do a bit of a study on it to come to an understanding of it and just see how it fit into the picture. The idea of "ensue" in relationship to peace is; having established it, which may take considerable time and effort, now "enjoy and live with the results of it".

Having grown up in a society and world, that is contrary to the "things" found in Biblical content, and being influenced and conditioned by that world; with my family as a blessed exception, we have some work to do in the **[Romans 12:2] "renewing of our minds" to be transformed out of this world and its ways of contrariness in order to adjust to this new way of thinking.** We do have in **verse 7, the "peace of God" and in verse 9, the "God of peace"** as a promise for "thinking on these things" in the process of, **[Proverbs 4:23] "Keeping your heart with all diligence; conditioned with the Word of Peace so that peaceful issues of life may develop in it and flow naturally out of it".**

It is good to know that in a world that is filled with turmoil, strife, and stress, that Jesus has given us the ability, freedom, and desire, to condition our minds, hearts, and lives with the things that tend to "peace" for the glory and pleasure of God and our own temporal and eternal benefit. **[2 Corinthians 13:11], "Finally, brethren, farewell: Be perfect, be of good comfort, be of one mind, live in peace; and the God of peace shall be with you.**

Now let's turn to an area of peace that should provide inspiration for any and all who are interested in enjoying this thing called "peace". **[Isaiah 26:3-4] "Thou wilt keep him in PERFECT PEACE, whose mind is stayed on thee: because he trusteth in thee. Trust ye in the Lord for ever: for in the Lord Jehovah is everlasting strength".** Now we have the promise of "perfect peace", if we meet the condition of obtaining it. This condition is to **"keep our minds stayed, fixed, on the "God of peace", loving the word for GREAT**

PEACE, [Psalms 119:165], delighting in and meditating on God's word [Psalms 1:2], [studying, 2 Timothy 2:15], and [doing his word, James 1:22], instead wallowing in the things of this world and its contrary ways that oppose God, his righteousness, holiness, and peace, thus do we "oppose ourselves", **[2 Timothy 2: 12]. [Colossians 3:2] "Set your affection on things above, not on things on the earth".** It is extremely important to learn to, **[Proverbs 3:5-6.] "Trust in the Lord with all thine heart; and lean not unto thine own understanding. In all thy ways acknowledge him, and he shall direct thy paths".** It makes it very desirable to keep our mind "stayed" on him when we realize that we can place our entire being, present, past, and future in his hands, trusting in him for our total well-being, knowing that his goodness and mercy will be our portion forever. **[Matthew 6:21] [Luke 12:34] "For where your treasure is, there will your heart be also".**

In growing older and realizing we have, in the normal course of life, less time than we used to have, we begin to understand that this *"peace" is in fact, a beautiful and necessary treasure.* This that we can enjoy with what time we do have left, we could have enjoyed much earlier in life, alleviating much anxiety, worry, stress, and possibly resulting sicknesses, including ulcers, had we been properly taught and indoctrinated in this pursuit of Godliness early on. As we study and learn about this majestic, creative, loving God, this "God of peace" that is totally devoted to us and our good, it should be very easy for a person, who is in the process of mind renewal, to fall deeply in love with him. As that process takes place, he becomes your "ultimate treasure" and your heart naturally gravitates to him and you find yourself desiring more of him in **"all his fullness", [Ephesians 3:13-21].** This is a natural result of **"setting our affection on things above and not on things on the earth", [Colossians 3:2].**

As we begin to see Jesus through the Holy Spirit taught, revealed word, we also begin to see God and to know him with a deeper and more fervent appreciation and intimacy. **[John 8:19; 14:7], "If ye had known me, ye should have known my Father also: and from henceforth ye know him, and have seen him". [1 John 3:2] "Beloved, now are we the sons of God, and it doth not yet appear what we shall be: but we know that, when he shall appear, we shall be like him; for we shall see him as he is".** This particular scripture has a tremendous amount of significance of its own. It seems to imply both a present and future series of events pertaining to the seeing, knowing, revealing, understanding, etc. of the Godhead through both physical seeing, and the mental comprehension, perceiving, and understanding. **[Ephesians 1:18], "The eyes of the understanding being enlightened" through the Holy Spirit revealing of the Word in our contemplation and meditation of it, enables us to "see", or perceive, some things that physically seeing some things will never reveal.**

You can see words such as, love, purity, righteousness, goodness, and a host of others, but that doesn't cause you to understand them until you can see the results of these things in action. It is then that we begin to gain the knowledge and understanding of what these things are, how they come to be, how they are attained to and shared, and the value of each in their individual and collective contributions to the over all enriching of life and life more abundantly. The wording of **[Isaiah 26: 3]** does not hold a specific command, that comes in verse 4, but it does present a principle which contains first, a promise, **"Thou wilt keep him in perfect peace"**, then the conditions of obtaining that promise, **"whose mind is stayed on thee: because he trusteth in thee"**. Verse 4 gives us the command as the principle of obedience continues, **"Trust ye in the Lord for ever"**: and concludes with the reason for being able to do this, which in itself should provide ample motivation for diligent, willing, obedience; **"for in the Lord Jehovah is everlasting strength"**.

There is a "law of obedience" stated here that is a strong cord running from cover to cover throughout God's Word. Much of the time it seems to be conspicuous by its absence which Adam and Eve set in motion in the Garden of Eden: from whence disobedience has been growing and intensifying every since. From the general condition of the world today, with the exception of the exceptions, it would seem that this disobedience and rebellion with the abominations that are a result has about reached its zenith and conclusion. Indeed the wages of sin are still death; and with the life gone out of the nations about all they have left is some sort of a survivalistic existence.

[Matthew 24:6-7; Mark 13:7-8], *"see that ye be not troubled*: **for all these things must come to pass, but the end is not yet"**. **[Luke 21:25-28]**, verse 28, **"And when these things begin to come to pass, THEN LOOK UP, AND LIFT UP YOUR HEADS, FOR YOUR REDEMPTION DRAWETH NIGH"**. **[Psalms 1:1; Deuteronomy 30:19]**, **"Blessed is the man, or nation, that walks in the whole counsel of God, that chooses life and blessing, instead of death and cursing, so that both they and their descendents shall live"**.

We cannot "see" the wind, but we know it's blowing because we can see and feel the physical affects and results of it. We today, can see the results of that which characterizes God the Father, God the Son, and God the Spirit, in action in all areas that pertain to him; but only then, if you have been taught and conditioned to see and understand. **[1 Corinthians 2: 14]**, **"But the natural man receiveth not the things of God: for they are foolishness to him: neither can he know them**

because they are spiritually discerned". I have a friend, Jim Justus, who has a saying, "you gotta learn to pay attention". It fits here. Those who saw him in his resurrected form did not even know him until he opened their eyes of understanding as to who he was, but this still did not reveal the scope of what he was, who he was, and the fullness of what he represented. That could only be seen and revealed through much study and revelation by way of the Holy Spirit as he teaches those who have eyes to see, ears to hear, and a heart and mind to understand. Such was the situation with Peter in **[Matthew 16:17] in his understanding of what the Father revealed to him concerning Jesus.**

All of this is contained in the conditioning and learning process that is needed to **[1Thessalonians 4:4], "know how to possess your vessel;** *yourself in conversation and conduct,* **in sanctification and honour" unto the Lord. [Proverbs 1:7] "The fear, reverencing, of the Lord is the beginning of knowledge: but fools despise wisdom and instruction".** These who refuse the instructions to possess their "vessels" accordingly, will never see nor understand. To begin with, they neither have the intelligence to reverence God nor are inclined to do so, thus is the "beginning of wisdom, knowledge, and understanding," beyond their perception and they despise them. But those of **[Matthew 5:6], who "hunger and thirst after righteousness shall be blessed and filled" and perfect peace shall be theirs.**

This is part of the process of the "renewing of the mind", determining and establishing value for the "things" that accompany salvation and doing always those "things" that please God, [Hebrews 6:9]-[John 8:29].

In **[Psalms 119:165]** we find some more interesting input concerning this treasure of "peace" which is virtually non-existent in our world today, nor in sufficient supply in the

Christian world. It reads **"Great peace have they which love thy law: and nothing shall offend them", or be a stumbling block to them.** In the 176 verses of the 119 th Psalm, there are only about six verses that do not contain a word that relates directly to the word "WORD". For this reason I do not hesitate to prefer to use the word "WORD" in preference to other words that make the relationship between them realistic. Others may disagree, so be it; it works for me. Personally I see a tremendous amount of mercy, grace, and forgiveness throughout the Old Testament and a considerable amount of law within the New Testament. Law and grace are both present in their respective applications to be used for the glory of God and the well being of all mankind in both Testaments.

A law used as a principle in the establishment of obedience, righteousness, holiness, purity, etc. cannot be disregarded simply because we are under grace and the law or principle establishing it is found in the Old Testament: **[2 Timothy 3:16]** still applies here. Grace was not given to replace obedience nor to allow and cover disobedience. **Loving the "word" implies and demands obedience to the word which begins with repentance, [Mark 1:15].** "Believe on the Lord Jesus Christ and thou shalt be saved, *and thy house*" [Acts 16:31]: this also implies and demands obedience to the word which begins with repentance that brings forth fruit meet for and, shows proof of, repentance. Violate this and you will not only, not experience "great peace", but no peace whatsoever. If you are experiencing strife, contentions, animosities, etc, in your life, home, and family etc, it is time to do some evaluating concerning the problems and their cause that is producing such devastating effects.

This also has national implications and concerns the condition of America today and what it will be tomorrow. The violation of God's word is commensurate with the rejecting, neglecting, and forgetting **[Hosea 4:6] of the law, word, of God,** which destroys individuals, families, churches, and nations. In **[Matthew 22:36-40]** we find some very important "law" being given here for our admonition, direction, and application. We have been set free through the administration of God's grace through Jesus Christ to be obedient to and obey the "law, the word of God". Grace indeed has a tremendous application and purpose here, but it was never intended to replace obedience to God's word, or his "law". Some laws apply; some do not. **[2 Timothy 2:15], "Study to show thyself approved unto God, a workman that needeth not to be ashamed,** *rightly dividing* **the word of truth". [Romans 8:2] "For the law of the Spirit of life in Christ hath made me free from the law of sin and death".** There are laws that need to be applied and laws that need to be set aside, but God's word, his love, mercy, and grace, repentance, and our obedience, are always applicable, never to be set aside. **Obedience IS NOT just a suggestion!**

Though I have used the KJV and have learned to appreciate and love it over the years, I have no hesitation in using some other versions of the Bible for reference and assistance in my studies. Occasionally I find some wording that is preferable to some in the KJV. An instance of this is in **[Ps. 119:165]** used in this writing concerning the word **"offend"** where the words **"shall be a stumbling block to them"** provide a much deeper implication of our responsibility of spiritual strength and stability. Sin itself is, or rather should always be offensive to the Christian but never be allowed to be a stumbling block. I do not, however, have the hang-ups over the, thee's, thou's, and thy's of the KJV that some people seem to have. To me it gives the KJV a kind of majestic aura and elegant class that other versions have lost in their more modern translations. I enjoy this same majestic aura and class in Paul's greetings to the people in his letters to the churches he is writing to, **"Grace to you and PEACE from God our Father and the Lord Jesus**

Christ". It just might do us some good to crucify our stupid pride and adopt some of the things we find in this WORD we claim to believe in and follow. We want all the benefits but we don't seem to be quite so adamant about the required obedience, examples, and fruitful suggestions for the obtaining of those benefits.

Certainly a more intimate relationship with the word would provide a more intimate relationship with the peace that seems at times so elusive. Some how or another we have gotten the attitude that grace will take care of it all, including our uncorrected inconsistencies. What a shabby, ungrateful way to treat God and abuse this beautiful gift of his amazing grace. Its no wonder "peace" is in such short supply in many professing Christian lives; more professing than practicing, I suspect. I also suspect that there would be less requirement and stress, for our counselors if there were more individual determination and commitment to **"keep thy heart with all diligence" so it can issue forth the life that God intended for it to produce.**

It is good to be in "church" and attend Sunday School, and absolutely essential for many, but the prerequisite for being a **[2 Corinthians 5:17] new creature in Christ, saved by grace is to be "in Christ". To be "in Christ" is to abide in his word, in him, and he in you. [John 14:23] "Jesus answered and said unto him, if a man love me, he will keep my words: and my Father will love him, and we will come unto him, and make our abode,** establish residence, **with him".** This is the essence of "being in Christ". **[John 8:29] "He that sent [called, sanctified, commissioned, ordained, etc.], me IS WITH ME: the FATHER HATH NOT LEFT ME ALONE;** *for I do always those things that please him".* I will have to confess that I do not always keep my part of the deal as I should but that is where God's grace really comes into its own. However, I am constantly and consistently working on this. I have been given to understand that *"perfect practice makes perfect"*.

As I learn to embrace an attitude of love and obedience toward Jesus, with resultant conversation and conduct, I find that I don't put such a strain on grace. I am learning to maintain its coverage and use for that for which it is intended rather than misuse and abuse it even though it does the job perfectly whenever I fail. *An in-depth realization of this translates into perfect, great, and wonderful "peace".* It is good to give thanks unto the Lord, to express attitudes of love in words, but this must be accompanied with thanks and gratitude translated into a life style of conduct and behavior, of loving, willing obedience to God for his glory, honour, and pleasure, **[Deuteronomy 28: 47], "Serving the Lord thy God with joyfulness and gladness of heart, for the abundance of all things".** It is good to serve God, **it is better and best to serve him with the proper attitude, working righteousness, as in [Acts 10:35].** As we learn and apply this we will enjoy his constant presence, **[Philippians 4:7] "And the peace of God, which passeth all understanding, shall keep your hearts and minds through Christ Jesus".**

NOTES

NOTES

VIII.   PEOPLE

People, I'm not opposed to them. I'm one of them; that's how I know them so well. However, general observation of humanity and a study of their history provide quite an accurate accounting of this creature that, *by his own hand,* is not what he was created to be. That alone gives us considerable insight into the questionable quality of his intelligence. I'm all for people. It's the traits and characteristics that identify them as to what the majority of them have become that is so disgusting. Three main ones seem to stand out; stupidity, ignorance, and idiocy. That is not the way God created us, so how did we get to this deplorable condition, and with the way out available, why do people insist in remaining in such a despicable state of being?

Lets face it, this world, indeed, America, "the land of the free and the home of the brave" didn't get to it's degraded condition by the use of Godly wisdom, intelligence, understanding, and knowledge of the things of God. **[Daniel 12:4] tells us that, "even to the time of the end: many shall run to and fro, and knowledge shall be increased".** Knowledge has increased by leaps and bounds concerning the things of this earth, and man wouldn't have been able to do the magnificent things he has done if it weren't for the abilities that God created in him to learn, develop, and do these things. Unfortunately we don't seem to have developed the wisdom and intelligence to understand how to use that knowledge for the uses God intended; to bring him glory and honor and benefit humanity over the long haul.

Unfortunately in all his efforts to "feather his own nest" with the things of this world, he neglected to cultivate a substantial knowledge of God, his goodness and abundance of love, mercy, and grace. In attaining to this knowledge of God, man needed to gain some of the knowledge that God has, including knowledge of the adversary of his soul, which is learned by a study of God's Word and paying attention to the world around him. There is considerable information available within God's storehouse of knowledge about this individual, Satan, Lucifer, the devil, liar, deceiver, etc, etc. Man has discounted his existence and remained ignorant of him even while being enslaved by him. In his lack of knowledge, **[Hosea 4:6]**, concerning this destroyer; man has willingly, and unwittingly served him throughout the **ages without even regarding the fact he was, and is, being destroyed from morning to evening, continually, for ever, [Job 4: 20]**.

Man became too distracted in his intense pursuit of fun, games, excitement, pleasure, and becoming successful by worldly standards; or just occupied by putting beans on the table. This alone was to be a difficult chore for some. Man was created as something special to do wonderful things for God's glory, but he did not retain that specialty and now we have governmental entities and educators trying to convince him that he is only a developed blob of something that began on the ocean floor. He never gained the wisdom and understanding to intelligently manage and govern the vast amount of knowledge he attained to, nor the material wealth of God's creation. Our worst enemies are indeed, "those of our own countrymen". The insidious idiocy of this whole scenario is beyond description and understanding. How beings that claim to be intelligent can be so incredibly stupid is mind boggling.

From the standpoint of mentality, he embraced stupidity, ignorance, and idiocy, and as a result he is destroying his world little by little, although the speed and intensity of this is increasing at an alarming rate, one culture and one nation at a time, beginning with his own life. Great nations have come and gone throughout the ages past because of the three destructive traits of man and he still hasn't learned his lessons. You'll have to agree, that is about as stupid as you can get. Being of the human race, I to, have fallen victim to these three traits from time to time and it bothers me to think that I may even live long enough to experience one or more of them again before I'm gone. That in itself could be a bit depressing. **[Job 5:7] tells us "man is born unto trouble, as the sparks fly upward"**.

It seems that man can't get above the three destructive traits, so he just keeps wallowing in his foolishness, **building his own fires of trouble and walking in the sparks he has created for himself, [Isaiah 50:11]**. Thank God for the exceptions. Thank God for his provision of deliverance from such a state of rebellion and the foolishness of **"the sin which doth so easily beset us", [Hebrews 12:1]**. *However, God has made a way for deliverance, and his name is Jesus.* God sent deliverers to the nation of Israel time after time when their stupidity got them into trouble and he has sent us Jesus Christ to bail us out of ours and all we have to do is **[Mark 1: 15], "repent and believe the gospel"**, *and believe it strong enough to be obedient and live by it.* The implication here is that to believe it and be obedient to it will require studying it to find out precisely what we are to believe in and be obedient to. This is emphasized in **[2 Timothy 2: 15], "Study to show thyself approved unto God, a workman that needeth not to be ashamed, rightly dividing the word of truth"**.

Throughout the Bible, God is characterized and described in many ways to which we will never be nor attain to. However, there are some things about him that are contained in his **[Genesis 1:26] image and likeness that we are to tap into, retain, and develop for his pleasure and glory and our own well being.** He is the God of Wisdom, Understanding, Knowledge, and certainly Intelligence. God is certainly the God of infinite ability in any and all areas and things. Man, as a result of his disobedience and rejection of God has shown a great propensity for his natural stupidity, ignorance, idiocy, and foolishness, all of which have become very characteristic of his nature, condoning and promoting sinful practices. These are things he didn't have to learn, they were just there, descriptive of his sinful nature and even as Christian's they still rear their ugly heads up at the most inopportune times. This is the way iniquity works. It is spoken of Satan himself; **[Ezekiel 28:15], "Thou wast perfect in thy ways from the day that thou wast created, till INIQUITY WAS FOUND IN THEE".** Our relationship with iniquity is identical to Satan's, **it is found in us:** we didn't have to go to some particular place to find it and it will tag along and plague us unless it is cast out and destroyed. This can only be accomplished through Jesus Christ our Lord and Saviour.

It may well have been introduced by Satan but man has certainly kept it going. Once he fired the starting gun, we took over from there. We have a very accurate description of mankind, his foolishness, and God's provision for his redemption and reconciliation in **[Ephesians 2:1-10]. Verses 1-3, "And you hath he quickened, who were dead in trespass and sins; Wherein in times past ye walked according to the course of this world, according to the prince of the power of the air, the spirit that now worketh in the children of disobedience: Among whom we all had our conversation in times past in the lusts of our flesh, fulfilling the desires of the flesh and of the mind; and were by nature the children of wrath, even as others".**

Iniquity has abounded and flourished in mankind. **Verse's 4-10, "BUT GOD, who is rich in mercy, for his great love where with he loved us, Even when we were dead in sins, hath quickened us together with Christ, [by grace are ye saved]; And hath raised us up together, and made us sit together in heavenly places in Christ Jesus, that in,** *and throughout,* **the ages to come he might show the exceeding riches of his grace in his kindness toward us through Christ**

Jesus. For by grace are ye saved through faith; and that not of yourselves: it is the gift of God: Not of works lest any man should boast. For we are his workmanship; created in Christ Jesus unto good works, which God hath before ordained that we should walk in them".

Though many are still keeping the iniquity going and inventing new methods of doing so, there are some who are not. Thank God for these exceptions. Sin and iniquity will, as an invader, still pop up on occasion to be quickly dealt with and destroyed, but it is not a part of our new divine nature. Thank you Jesus, for your deliverance! **[Matthew 7:13-14], "Enter ye in at the strait gate: for wide is the gate, and broad is the way that leadeth to destruction, and many there be which go in thereat: because strait is the gate and narrow is the way which leadeth unto life, and few there be that find it". [Deuteronomy 30: 19],"Therefore choose life, that both thou and thy seed may live".** Once again, thank you Lord for the few exceptions. It is indeed sad that there are not many, many, more.

People; they come from all walks of life, from the four corners of the earth, in all shapes and sizes, nationalities, colors, and creeds. Whatever the various differences may be, they have one thing in common; SIN. **[Romans 3:23], "For all have sinned and come short of the glory of God", and all are in need of repentance of this sin unto salvation through Jesus Christ. [Mark 1:14-15], "Now after John was put in prison, Jesus came into Galilee, preaching the gospel of the kingdom of God, And saying, The time is fulfilled, and the kingdom of God is at hand: repent ye and believe the gospel". [John 3: 3-8], verse 7; "Ye must be born again". [2 Peter 3:9], "The Lord is not slack concerning his promise, as some men count slackness; but is longsuffering to us-**

ward, not willing that any should perish, *but that all should come to repentance".*

There are many other scriptures referring to the need for repentance from sin which should give us a clue to the absolute necessity for it. Though grace is available at all times, it doesn't take effect until heart felt repentance is executed. Many attempt to avoid repentance and become part of the crowd of whom it is said**, [Matthew 15:8; Mark 7:6], "This people honoureth me with their lips; but their heart is far from me". [Acts 17:30], "And the times of this ignorance God winked at; but now** *commandeth all men every where to repent".*

[Acts 2:38], "Then Peter said unto them, Repent and be baptized every one of you in the name of Jesus Christ for the remission of sins, and ye shall receive the gift of the Holy Ghost". Repentance is the front door you have to open and go through in order to avail yourself of the abundance of the Lord that he, by his grace, has made available to us. At any rate, dealing with sin in a conscientious, Bible orientated manner would be a good practice to get into. You will need to know how to do that along the way as the deceiver never gives up and is constantly setting traps to catch some unwary Christian; therefore **[1 Peter 5:8], "Be sober, be vigilant; because your adversary the devil, as a roaring lion, walketh about, seeking whom he may devour", and rest assured, if you are a Christian, you are his target.** He has already had the sinner, the non-Christian, for lunch whether they are aware or not, whether they even care or not. **[Hosea 4:20], "They are destroyed from morning to evening: they perish for ever without any regarding it". [Proverbs 4: 26], "Ponder, [regard, give attention to] the path of thy feet, and let thy ways be established". [Proverbs 3:5-6], "Trust in the Lord with all thine heart; and lean not to thy own understanding. In all thy ways acknowledge him,** *and he shall direct thy paths".*

Considering the gross lack of proper Bible based teaching and training that is left unattended to throughout our nation in all elements of our society, including the church and our governmental leaders, it is no wonder our nation is in the state of deterioration it finds itself. There are a few exceptions that may make a difference in a marriage or hopefully a family, but not to the extent that is needed to rebuild America. We have no "mighty men" in our civil leadership areas, only scoffers and scorners of righteousness who are allowed to continue in their idiocy. They have their rights, in their pernicious ways, infecting the whole of society, with their malignancy, and the "intelligence" of human government without God, has allowed them their right to do so. The guaranteeing of such dubious rights is one of the things that man in his ignorance has considered in the recognizing of America for her greatness. Intelligence with a little simple common sense would forbid the exercising and practicing of such destructive "rights". Once again does William Shakespeare come to mind, **"What fools ye mortals be".** Mankind has indeed demonstrated his profound foolishness throughout the ages with that foolishness proceeding into idiocy and absolute stupidity and advancing in intensity with increasing shame and disgrace, **[Hosea 4: 7] As they were increased, so they sinned against me: therefore will I change their glory into shame".**

The deplorable condition of our entire world is vivid testimony to that fact. There are of course a few exceptions to this however, but as to the moral, ethical, and psychological condition, there are few exceptions to be found. As to the spiritual, one would have to identify what spiritual source, religion, or belief is being referred to as they are many and varied. Contrary to a popular belief being voiced from time to time, *not all roads lead to heaven.* **[Genesis 1:1], "In the beginning God created heaven and earth"** and God alone can and has made it possible for man to ascend to heaven and created the way to do so through Jesus Christ our Saviour. **[John 14:6], "Jesus saith unto him, I am the way, the truth, and the life: no man cometh to the Father, but by me". [Matthew 7: 13-14], "Enter ye in at the strait gate: for wide is the gate, and broad is the way, that** *leadeth to destruction, and many there be which go in thereat:* **Because strait is the gate , and narrow is the way, which leadeth to life, and** *few* **there be that find it".**

There are many on the broad way that leads to destruction in comparison to the few on the narrow way that leads to life, but the narrow way is the only road to life and heaven. There are and will continue to be many who would argue that point, however they will have to take that up with God; he is the one who designed it to be thus. Don't argue with me, I'm just agreeing with God and attempting to present it as he has presented it to us.

You may disagree with me all you wish; it will make no difference to me or to you. Disagree with God if you so choose, it still won't make any difference to me, however, it may well make a temporal and eternal difference to you whether you like it or not.

NOTES

NOTES

IX. LIFE OR EXISTENCE

"The thief cometh not, but to steal, and to kill, and to destroy: I am come that they might have life, and that they might have it more abundantly", [John 10:10]. Having a life filled with meaning and purpose versus an empty, shallow existence is dependant upon the development of the mind and the resultant interests pursued. Value must be perceived to be seen and understood to provide inspiration followed by an intelligent response to the value perceived, even if not yet completely understood. A person may well enjoy, to a certain limited degree, an existence of sinful indulgences and excesses. The world is filled with this type of thing with many willing participants, as a person embraces a lifestyle of an "if it feels good do it" culture.

Everything that is sought for and indulged in for the purpose of satisfying the carnal desires of a very shallow non-thinking self that is willing to sacrifice their very being to the gods of fun and games, pleasures and thrills, is an exercise of futility. **[Job 4:20], refers to this as being "destroyed from morning to evening: they perish forever without any regarding it.** Shakespeare puts it this way; **"What fools ye mortals be."** I'll have to agree with him. Nero fiddled while Rome burned. Somehow I can't help but see a likeness with all the fiddling around that Americans are involved with and not taking God seriously from government to and including the governed. Verse 21 continues, **"Doth not their excellency which is in them go away?"** They die, even without wisdom. [Job 5: 6-7], **"Although affliction cometh not forth of the dust, neither doth trouble spring forth out of the ground; yet man is born unto trouble as the sparks fly upward".** [Isaiah 50: 11], **"Behold, all ye that kindle a fire,** *that compass yourselves about with sparks:* **walk in the light of your fire, and in the** *sparks that ye have kindled.* **This shall ye have of mine hand; ye shall lie down in sorrow"**. There is certainly an analogy here connecting Nero's fiddling while Rome burns with our fiddling around with the fires of sin and iniquity bringing about the destruction of our own lives, families, churches, whatever, thus the destruction of America, our beloved homeland. Our governing system has failed us completely in the meeting of their ruling responsibilities and duties. Crow and argue about the greatness of the democratic system of government if you wish; it still remains inadequate to govern a nation without enlisting and obedience to God's counsel and input, **[Psalms 127: 1], "Except the Lord build the house, they labor in vain that build it: except the Lord keep the city, the watchman waketh but in vain"**.

It's a tragic situation, this stupidity that man is drowning himself in, as he struggles through an existence in rejection and neglect of God only to die, even without wisdom as he watches his beloved homelands crumble and disintegrate because he doesn't have the wherewithal, the right stuff, to prevent it. There is much temporal pleasure to be experienced in a shallow unproductive life that remains undeveloped because of the consistent refusal to accept the challenge of the renewing of the mind, the re-creating of the mentality, the diligent keeping of the heart, thus the enriching of the entire being. Consequently there is more heartache and misery experienced than there is pleasure.

I am utterly amazed how some unsavory wretch without any sense of decency, with a mind for aggression, can rise to power, conscript the populace for his army, proceed to kill and plunder other countries for nothing other than selfish reasons, losing multitudes of his own countrymen in his efforts, and be recognized and hailed as a great leader. Surely, man's sense of values without God's guidance, values and standards, are completely down the drain, and he doesn't even have the sense to know it. **[Isaiah 5: 24], "Therefore as the fire devoureth the stubble, and the flame consumeth the chaff, so their root shall be as rottenness, and their blossom shall go up as dust: because they have cast away the law of the Lord of hosts, and despised the word of the Holy One of Israel".**

This evil, foolish undisciplined, unrestrained, kind of conduct without knowledge of God and his Word of wisdom, knowledge, and understanding brings discord and havoc in a society and culture and has been known to destroy entire nations. America is trapped in this idiocy today, **[Job 4: 20-21], "They are destroyed from morning to evening: they perish forever without any regarding it. Doth not their excellency which is in them go away? They die, even without wisdom".**

As this is happening, our illustrious leaders in all their positions and capacities haven't got a clue as to the solution to all these dilemma's, and the problems increase and intensify while they sit around in their committees and groups and get paid big bucks just to engage in endless meaningless, dialogue and discussion about it all, then adjourn and proceed to the golf course, the bar, or wherever, and the world marches on in its iniquity and destructiveness. We keep playing our fiddles, indulging ourselves in our fun, games, and pleasures as the fires of iniquity continue to burn and destroy as anti-God, anti-Christ, anti-decency groups and organizations of our own countrymen keep the fires burning with their abominations and destructive filth. **[Isaiah 5: 13-16], "Therefore my people are gone into captivity, because they have no knowledge: and their honorable men are famished, and their multitudes are dried up with thirst. Therefore hell hath enlarged herself, and opened her mouth without measure: and their glory, and their multitude, and their pomp, and he that rejoiceth,** *shall descend into it.* **And the mean man shall be brought down, and the mighty man shall be humbled, and the eyes** of the lofty shall be humbled: BUT the Lord of hosts shall be exalted in judgment, and God that is holy shall be sanctified in righteousness".

It is of extreme importance that we study to learn to think the way God thinks, having Godlike thoughts, so that our ways may become more conformed to his ways. The pleasures of this world are at the very best temporary to varying degrees and are extremely good at concealing the inevitable curses of death and destruction that follow close on the heels of the thoughtless indulgences of such pleasures, by diverting the complete attention to the anticipated pleasures. The shallow, undeveloped mind does not have the ability of the trained, developed mind to perceive the extent of the curses of sinful pleasures that may well be immediate, continual, and eternal, and in many cases, they are exactly that. The foolish neither regard this nor take it to heart, and the wealth of the wealthy cannot them out of it, nor deliver them from it. *Contrast this with the delight and meditation of the righteous,* **[Psalms 1:2] and the results promised in verse 3. [Psalms 1: 1-3], "Blessed is the man who walketh not in the counsel of the ungodly, nor standeth in the way of sinners, nor sitteth in the seat of the scornful; But his *delight is in the law of the Lord;* and in his law, his Word, doth he meditate day and night. And he shall be like a tree planted by the rivers of water, that bringeth forth his fruit in his season; and his leaf shall not wither; and whatsoever he doeth shall prosper".** It is tragic that so few understand the significance, majesty, content, and substance of these three scriptures.

With an obsession of anticipated pleasure overwhelming the mind and no concept of the curses that follow, and the penalties to be paid; it is exceedingly difficult if not impossible for a person to make a proper discriminatory choice between indulgence and non-indulgence unless the mind is extremely well disciplined and conditioned to Biblical counsel and intelligence. Even then the necessary follow-thru is quite often absent. If a person is unaware of, and thus unacquainted with a correct, different choice and the value of that choice, they will naturally remain in the rut of self destruction and enjoy whatever pleasure they can find there that contributes to that self destruction. ***How tremendously important is the concept of the "renewed mind and the diligently kept heart", for deliverance from the enslavement of the world with its deceit and treachery.* [Ephesians 4: 14], "That we be no more children, tossed to and fro, and carried about with every wind of doctrine, by the sleight of men, and cunning craftiness, whereby they lie in wait to deceive".**

A correct perception and analyzing of a choice that must be made, and the overall value of that choice and the result can and often helps lead a person to abhor today what they indulged in, practiced, and enjoyed yesterday. We must understand **[John 14: 26], "But the Comforter, which is the Holy Ghost, whom the Father will send in my name, he shall teach you all things, and bring all things to your remembrance, whatsoever I have said unto you"**, is always applicable and that class is always in session. **[John 15:3], "Now ye are clean through the [applied] word that I have spoken unto you"**.

This is necessary for proper contribution for growth and development of life and life more abundantly. This is wisdom and intelligence and it does takes time and discipline, following on the action of **[Mark 1:15], "repentance and believing the gospel unto obedience"**.

It is virtually impossible for a young person who has been totally indoctrinated in the non-Biblical influences of this world to make an intelligent choice between Biblical teachings and worldly pursuits. It is difficult to impossible to discern between good and evil, right and wrong when all you've been taught is wrong and it has been legalized, camouflaged, portrayed, and presented as right and legal, and has been accepted as such by a wayward society and bathed in the concept of relativity. Don't get me wrong, I believe in relativity. I believe that everything is relative, **To God's Word,** and must be weighed by its truth, absolutes, values, and standards. If you can't or won't agree with that, that's your problem, deal with it as best you can, but I will not change my mind just to accommodate you. **God's Word still stands as supreme above all that is in contrast to it, or opposes it. [Matthew 24: 35; Mark 13: 31; Luke 21: 33], "Heaven and earth shall pass away, but my words shall not pass away"**.

This too, you will have to deal with, don't wait until it is to late. **[2 Peter 3:9], "The Lord is not slack concerning his promise, as some men count slackness; but is longsuffering to us-ward, not willing that any should perish, *but that all should come to repentance"*.** Again, don't wait until it is to late. **"Now is the accepted time, now is the day of salvation", [2 Corinthians 6:2].**

Many women who have had abortions thought it was alright based on the worlds wisdom of legalizing it but never realized the adverse trauma they would suffer that the world could not prepare them to deal with later. Nor does the world and its atheistic, anti-Christ, unloving, advocates care. This kind of secularist thinking has been a great travesty in much of our educational system, but certainly not limited to our educational system. It seems as though this gross error of judgment has taken root and produced it evil fruit in every facet of our society including, unfortunately some of our more liberal churches where there is no longer a **"hungering and thirsting after righteousness", consequently, neither is there any filling or manifestation of such fullness", [Matthew 5: 6].** However, this is not surprising considering man's propensity, lust, hunger, and thirst for sin due to his sinful nature.

This erroneous input becomes a personal lifestyle, culture, and custom and it takes more than a bunch of legislated laws, rules, and regulations by those who were instrumental in initiating such erroneous input to begin with to change the life that has been adversely affected by such nonsense and idiocy. It takes super natural intervention by the sovereign God who can infiltrate the heart and mind of such an infected person with the living Holy Spirit, assisting them in a change of direction, to convince and reveal to such a person **"a new and living way", [Hebrews 10: 20]. This is the way of joy unspeakable and full of glory, [1Peter 1:8]. Jesus was, is, and always will be, the truth, the life, and this new and living way, [John 14:6].**

We are all wrong who have rejected God and his word, and it is wrong to neglect to study and learn his ways after we have accepted him as we continue to live in a world that teaches rebellion and rejection. We will continue to live in error to the degree in which we are disobedient and neglectful of the diligent love, study, meditation, and adherence to God's word, even though we have set our hearts to obedience. **Thank God for his patience, understanding, forgiveness, and his amazing grace that is always available as we repent, are forgiven, and grow in his teaching, love, and guidance, always endeavoring to remain rooted and grounded in his word and faith.**

The very admonishment to grow in the grace and knowledge of our Lord and Saviour Jesus Christ implies a beginning and a long process of maturing in which many mistakes and instances of disobedience may well be experienced, **repented of and washed away by the blood of Jesus, being corrected and cleansed by the applied word that he has spoken to us, [John 15: 3].** It is part of the process of maturing in Christ. However as long as the heart is right in its desire to please him, this cannot and will not be considered as rebellion against God as a right attitude and correct desires will gradually bring the correct conduct into being, although a baptism of repentance must be maintained. **It is imperative however, that we maintain diligence in the keeping and guarding of our hearts as we experience the process of the renewing of our minds if we expect to enjoy life versus existence, [Proverbs 4:23]. God's grace is sufficient for us in our struggles of maturing in Him. [1 John 2:1-3],"My little children, these things write I unto you, that ye sin not. And if any man sin, we have an advocate with the Father, Jesus Christ the righteous: And he is the propitiation for our sins: and not for ours only, but also for the sins of the whole world. And hereby we do know that we know him, if we keep his commandments".**

Let's consider these as growing pains. We have them in the natural life and we will have them in the spiritual life. We will, however, move closer to perfection in our conduct as we learn perfection in our desires to **"please God in all that we think, say, and do"**. We must learn to assist, and will naturally encourage one another in our journey to maturity and the **"resurrection of excellency"**. Thank God for his faithfulness and patience during our journey of development in him as he administers and multiplies his love, mercy, and grace to us.

NOTES

NOTES

X. THE EXCEPTIONS

Thank God for the exceptions. In light **of [Matthew 7:13-14], "Enter ye in at the strait gate: for wide is the gate, and broad is the way, that leadeth to destruction, and many there be which go in thereat: Because strait is the gate, and narrow is the way, which leadeth unto life, and few there be that find it."** These **"few"** of verse 14 are the ones I refer to as the **EXCEPTIONS** versus the many of verse 13 which, unfortunately, are the norm. We may, in our post-modern jargon refer to them as the minority versus the majority. Of a certainty, this is a case where the majority does not rule, except by default under a democratic system of government. It may be the best, but without God at the helm for guidance, counsel, and direction, though it may flourish for a time, it to will go the way of all other nations who rejected God; **[Isaiah 5: 24], "Therefore as the fire devoureth the stubble, and the flame consumeth the chaff, so their root shall be as rottenness, and their blossom shall go up as dust: because they have cast away the law of the Lord of hosts, and despised the word of the Holy One of Israel".**

However, the question of who is actually *"calling the shots"* in our post modern world is another topic for another time. This may well be a good thing as well as very tragic: a good thing considering who has established the rules for operation and conduct of his creation, and will eventually set it all straight, and reward or punish according to such conduct. The results of who is presently and temporarily allowed to *"call the shots"*, is certainly questionable because of the ungodly nature of the majority that has, and is bringing shame and disgrace on our "land of the free and the home of the brave. However, this is also why it is so very tragic, for this ungodly "Democratic" majority is in the process of destroying themselves and the nation along with them, **bringing shame and disgrace to America** but, **[2 Peter 3:9], "The Lord is not willing that any should perish, but that all should come to repentance."** Unfortunately God is not getting what he wants from this majority, nor does this majority understand what they really need for life and life more abundantly: **"the many that go in at the wide gate and travel the broad way that leadeth to destruction".**

It seems that there are only a "few exceptions" who find the strait gate and walk the narrow way which leads to life everlasting in comparison to **the many, the multitudes who are the norm which travel the way of the wide gate and broad way that leads to destruction, [Matthew 7: 13-14].** These "many" certainly consists of those referred to in **[Isaiah 5:14]** with some preceding and following verses in reference to them for whom **"hell hath enlarged herself, and opened her mouth without measure: and their glory, their multitude, and their pomp, and he that rejoiceth, shall descend into it".** These are those who in their foolishness have, **[Isaiah 5: 24]**, **"cast away the law of the Lord of hosts, and despised the word of the Holy One of Israel",** who may well be included among those that **"oppose themselves", [2 Timothy 2: 25].**

It is absolutely amazing how that we can have such a detailed history of man's rebellion and rejection of God and the results of such stupidity, and still insist on making the same ridiculous mistakes in dishonoring God unto our own demise and destruction. There is no doubt that to some degree, but in different areas, we are all guilty of such nonsense and outright stupidity. If it were not for the amazing grace of God, there would none of us be saved. We find in **[Ephesians 2:1-3]** a general description of humanity, those who were dead in trespass and sin, but who, through the blood of Jesus by God's grace, and have been redeemed; now becoming Christians and on to the, **[2 Corinthians 5:17], position of being** *"new* *creatures in Christ, saved by the grace of God"* who have a totally different description of who and what they are with a new destiny as seen in **[Ephesians 2:4-10]. [Romans 1:21-32] gives a much more specific and detailed accounting of man before his repentance and believing the gospel, [Mark 1:15].**

For those interested, or not interested, which ever the case may be, you are invited and encouraged to study and review this portion of scripture, along with the rest of the Bible. Nevertheless, in this portion I am sure you will find something that should make you extremely grateful for the provision of salvation that God has so lovingly and gracefully provided for us through the cleansing power of the blood of Jesus.

For those who wallow in the sins of unbelief who claim they do not believe in the Bible and its gospel message of deliverance, redemption and reconciliation, you've got a tragic, eternal problem on your hands that only Jesus can cure. He is waiting for you just on the other side of your choice, **your decision to "repent and believe the gospel", choosing life and blessing, [Mark 1: 15; Deuteronomy 30: 19].** There are other portions of scripture that provide some more detailed descriptions of the existence of the sinner, lost and out side of God's divine protection, but this portion in **[Romans 1:21-32]**: should suffice for prompting to further investigation.

This is not what we dwell on, however, but concern ourselves with **[Romans 2:4] "the goodness of God that leadeth thee to repentance" and learning to, as Jesus did, to [John 8:29] "do always those things that please God, studying, learning, embracing, and "doing", [Hebrews 6:9] those things that accompany salvation".** I am sure that these "things" in both instances will be pretty much the same, but it is extremely important to search these "things" out by **[Hebrews 11:6], "diligently seeking God" and [2 Timothy 2:15],** "diligently" studying to show thyself approved unto God, a workman that needeth not to be ashamed, rightly dividing the word of truth".

It is good to be an "exception", however, there are some very important qualifications in determining how efficient and effective an "exception" you will be. How efficient and effective do you want to be is a question you will have to answer for yourself? You might consider some Biblical counsel in this area in **[1 Corinthians 10:31], "Whether therefore ye eat, or drink, or WHATSOEVER ye do, do ALL to the glory of God."** This "whatsoever" and "all" pretty well covers "whatsoever" we will need to learn about in this doing that which is necessary to glorify God, which of course will be to our own benefit as well.

In the process of learning these "whatsoevers", we will need to understand the necessity of their application also. Learning is one thing, doing is entirely another. We can be diligent in our learning, but quite neglectful and sloppy in the application of what is learned and as a result we begin to lose what we learned. The principle of "use it, or lose it" applies here. It is good to know these "whatsoever things"; it is good to get them firmly set in your mind **[Romans 12:2], for their application in the formation of a fruitful lifestyle. [Galatians 5: 22-23] gives us a good place to start learning these "whatsoevers".** Bear in mind, however, that "joy and peace" are not actually things you do, but are results and rewards for learning and doing the other things, "The Fruit of the Spirit".

There are, however, many other things that would, and do qualify as "Fruit of the Spirit, such as faith, patience, kindness, courtesy, temperance, and then there is wisdom, understanding, knowledge, and one of my favorites because it seems to be in such short supply in our post-modern world, and is so desperately needed is, *"intelligence"*, **the state of the Biblically**

conditioned and renewed mind, [Romans 12:1-2]. If there were a good supply of intelligence and reasoning, **[Isaiah 1:18],** based on God's word being manifested and applied, we would be living in a different and much better world than we are today and no doubt living and enjoying, as individuals, different and better lives in a very blessed and prosperous nation.

Just learning and applying good manners, courtesy's, and consideration to others would be a vast improvement over Americas present psychological and spiritual atmosphere It is good that as individual exceptions, although in the minority, we can tap into this intimacy of relationship with God regardless of the condition of the national majority who shape the nation with their anti-God attitude and votes. However, with the non-Biblical conditioning and training of our young people, we have failed terribly to train and prepare any suitable candidates for leadership positions for our nation and people to choose from. Consequently we have to settle for what we get with our inferior systems of educational efforts where Christian Biblical principles, which the Christian exceptions learn and embrace, are despised and rejected, thanks to erroneous governmental imposed "separation of church and state".

This is primarily aimed at Biblical Christian teachings while allowances are being made to accommodate many contrary anti-Bible religions opposed to this Biblical set of principles that were employed in the forming and establishing of the foundation for our America and have been her strength and greatness for so long. This, however seems to have faded away into the fog of the past, the implementation and enforcement of the "separation concept" along with "political correctness", another governmental evil invention being largely contributive to this. Someday man will realize that **"Biblical Correctness"** trump's political correctness anytime, every time, and every place.

It is essential that we who are the exceptions need to be busy about our **[Luke 2:49] "Father's business" and blending our lives into his "thoughts and ways", [Isaiah 55:7-9].** If a person is interested in correcting their *mind malfunctions*, and reversing their *mentality meltdown*; the conditions prevalent in this world system, they will need to get into God's word and learn to think as he thinks, reason as he reasons so your thoughts will become his thoughts and finally your ways conforming to his ways of righteousness, holiness, and purity, etc. etc. You will never have an opportunity any greater than today for deciding to, **[Romans 12:2], "be not conformed to this world, but be transformed by the renewing of your mind, that ye may prove what is that good, and acceptable, and perfect will of God."**

There is nothing that can compare to realizing that there is a place; **[2 Corinthians 5:17-18], where you become a new creature "in Christ" saved by the grace of God.** The old garbage of sin is washed away, the old desires and practices begin to fall by the wayside and pass away as we exercise ourselves in doing God's word, and just the thought of them has a tendency to make you nauseas. **"Behold, all things become new and all these "new things" are of God, who hath reconciled us to himself by Jesus Christ, and hath given, committed, to us the ministry of reconciliation".** As these things are learned, studied, practiced and become the **"new abundance of the heart"** they will displace to old things, the old sinful abundance. We will enter into the process of creating a new heart and thus a new mind. An in- depth study of what these *"new things that are of God" consist of,* will give considerable inspiration and be of eternal value to the one who searches them out.

There is a whole [Hebrews 10:20] exciting, new, and living way [John10:10] of life and life more abundantly available for, whosoever will may come and avail themselves of that which God has made available to them through Jesus Christ our Lord and Saviour.

Thank you Jesus, it is good to be an exception, "delivered" from the things of this world, and being free to the, **[Colossians 3:2], "setting our affection on the things above, not on the things on the earth".** I will often use the phrase, **"Thank God for the exceptions,"** in my writings as it is, considering the condition of this world, good to know they are there, and to be one of them. I have recently, because of the absolute cleansing power of the blood of Jesus and the **"applied word of God", [John 15:3],** have had thoughts of how Jesus, through being the product of what is termed as the **immaculate conception**, proceeded to implement the plan whereby we might become the **immaculate exceptions**. We sing songs that testify to this cleansing power, so why not accept the challenge of living up to it as mature, God pleasing exceptions. Jesus speaks of them in **[Matthew 16:18] when he says, "that upon this rock, of truth, that I am who the Father has revealed to you that I am, I will build MY church, of immaculate exceptions, and the gates of hell shall not prevail against it."** There are those that may well disagree with me, but the word "immaculate" simply testifies to the cleansing power of the blood of Jesus which we don't hear much about anymore, **[John 8: 36], "If the son therefore shall make you free, ye shall be free indeed".**

This is the church made up of the "exceptions", some more immaculate than others in the process of maturing, but all under the cleansing power of the blood of Jesus, still learning, growing, developing, and maturing, that are found throughout this world, some in the past, some in the present, and some certainly yet to come, in the future, **[Acts 2:39], "those that are afar off"**. That has to be referring to us, who at that time were about 2000 years **"afar off"**. This church is made up of every tongue, tribe, nationality, and people, for Peter said in **[Acts 10:34-35], "Of a truth I perceive that God is no respecter of persons;** ***BUT in every nation he that feareth him, and worketh righteousness, is accepted with him"**. **Red, yellow, black, white, brown, or whatever, "he that feareth "reveres" him and worketh righteousness is accepted with him"**.

It is said, I believe, originally by a sports coach, that **"it is not what you teach that counts, but what you *emphasize* in your teachings that counts"**, again **"practice does not make perfect, perfect practice makes perfect"**. Although the whole Bible, the Word of God, is of great importance, **[2 Timothy 3:16-17], "All scripture is given by inspiration of God, and is profitable for doctrine, for reproof, for correction, for instruction in righteousness: That the man of God may be perfect, thoroughly furnished unto all good works"**. It is important that the *essentials of the Christian walk that characterize the "divine nature", the new and living way, such as the "Fruit of the Spirit", be emphasized.* If you are an "exception", I rejoice with you, if you are not, I invite you to join us at the foot of The Old Rugged Cross where Jesus died so that we might live in God's love and grace, and **"be seated together in Jesus Christ our Lord"**.

It is easy and a natural thing to do, to put things in the same category when viewing them with a non-discriminating eye and attitude, but this is incorrect and wrong due to the exceptions that are present but not considered. For instance: it would be wrong and inaccurate to include that which is good with that which is evil simply because of a similarity of exterior likeness or other similarities. So it is wrong to categorize the saint with the sinner simply because they are both of the human race and at a distance, look the same. It would be equally wrong to place all institutions of education teachers and professors in the same category, as some are morally correct in their presentations and some are total failures in the area of morals, mentally and spiritually and, as a result of this, have no business being allowed to teach impressionable young minds anything because their presentations will always be tempered with their immorality and degraded, worldly thinking. Then there are of course those who design the textbooks and those who approve them with their questionable contents, some of which are so out of line concerning decency, truth, and the essentials needed to be good citizens of any society and culture that they are of a degraded quality below even being worthy of question.

This is certainly a reflection on the moral character, mentality and intelligence of the book designers as well as those that approve them, and, or agree with them which is a reflection on the overall mentality of our America. There is, and always must necessarily be, a wide and definite schism between those who promote iniquitous worldly practices of rebellion in their opposition to God and the Christian Bible with its principles of righteousness and holiness. There can be no harmony, unity, fellowship etc, between light and darkness, between sin and Godliness. **[2 Corinthians 6:14], "Be ye not unequally yoked together with unbelievers: for what fellowship hath righteousness with unrighteousness? And what communion hath light with darkness"? [Ephesians 5:8-13], verses 11-12, "And have no fellowship with the unfruitful works of darkness, but rather reprove them,** *for it is a shame even to speak of those things which are done of them in secret*". This scripture very well establishes the boundaries of "tolerance" for the Christian. We have many who have disregarded these boundaries who conduct themselves according to their feelings and emotions rather than the wisdom, truth, and absolutes of God's word while still declaring themselves as Christians. However, God's agenda is still on track to accomplish its eternal purpose according to His will. **[1Peter 4: 17], "For the time is come that judgment must begin at the house of God: and if it first begin at us, what shall the end be of them that obey not the gospel of God"**.

We as Christians, definitely have an advantage here as nothing really seems to be done in secret anymore. Even the sex perverts, I'm not much on political correctness, come out in the open and in their arrogance flout their evil, abominations in the face of the American public and are protected by some weird application of law defending their "rights" to do so. It's something or other about "freedom of expression" of an idiotic nature encouraging the "if it feels good, do it idea, thus bringing more shame and disgrace on our nation and directly contributing to its decay and destruction. Isn't this amazing when the Christians are ruled against and forbidden to promote the Christian religion in public while the abominations mentioned above are promoted even in our so called institutions of higher education as well as being paraded on the streets of our cities and towns in defiance of all that is good and decent. But they have their "rights" that government guarantees them. Again I refer to and defer to Shakespeare, **"What fools ye mortals be"**!

Again we see practices that reflect on the mentality of our nation and **"our glory is being turned into shame by the increase of sin" in our midst, [Hosea 4:7]**. Once again I must thank God for the exceptions who stand on the Word of God in opposition against the abominations that are so blatantly committed against both God and man **by [2 Timothy 2:25] "those that oppose themselves", and bringing shame and disgrace on our America. [Hosea 4: 7], "As they were increased, so they sinned against me: therefore will I change their glory into shame"**.

When God is excommunicated, his law and his truth are also excommunicated; [Proverbs 28: 4-5; 29:9], "They that forsake the law praise the wicked: but they that keep the law, God's Word, contend with them. Evil men understand not judgment: but they that seek the Lord understand all things. When the righteous are in authority, the people rejoice: but when the wicked bear rule the people mourn". As I listen to the news today it seems that even the politicians are becoming discouraged about the general run of things. In reading the letters to the editor in the newspaper, people are constantly registering complaints about multitudes of indiscriminate indiscretions throughout the land, while they themselves may be contributing to them in erroneous lifestyles outside of God's counsel and direction.

It does make one wonder if people are as aware of personal indiscretions and the correcting of them within themselves as they are about others correcting their abominations that are causing mega-concerns and problems in the lives of others around them. Principles established in the Old Testament are not regarded by some Christian's as important because **"we are not under law but under grace".** Yet these same principles are reinforced and confirmed in the New Testament as they all establish the same concept of **"Obedience to God's Word and Will" in both the Old and New Testaments.**

How is it that these well meaning Christians read and hear, but do not comprehend that **[2 Timothy 3:16] teaches us that "ALL SCRIRTURE IS GIVEN BY INSPIRATION OF GOD, and is profitable for doctrine, for reproof, for correction, for instruction in righteousness: that the man of God may be perfect, thoroughly furnished unto all good works".** This, **"ALL SCRIPTURE"** by necessity would have to include the Old Testament as well as the New Testament.

Here are a few you might consider: **[Deuteronomy 10: 12-13], "And now, Israel,** *America, your name*, **what doth the Lord thy God require of thee, but to fear the Lord thy God, to walk in all his ways, and to love him, and to serve the LORD THY God with all thy heart and with all thy soul, to keep the commandments of the Lord, and his statutes, which I command thee this day for thy good?** This is a good one to start with. Now lets go to **[Jeremiah 4: 14, 18, 20, and 22], "O Jerusalem,** *America, your name*, **wash thine heart from wickedness, that thou mayest be saved. How long shall thy vain thoughts lodge within thee? 18-Thy way and thy doings have procured these things unto thee; this is thy wickedness, because it is bitter, because it reacheth unto thine heart. 20- Destruction upon destruction is cried; for the whole land is spoiled: suddenly are my tents, [towers [?], spoiled, and my curtains in a moment. 22- For my people is foolish, they have not known me; they are sottish,** [foolish and stupid] **children, and they have none understanding: they are wise to do evil,** *but to do good they have no knowledge"*.

Thank God for the exceptions who, through God's counsel and guidance, are bringing, at least, a little sense and stability to our great nation. **[Hebrews 6:1], "Let us go on unto perfection through exercising ourselves unto Godliness and holiness to being "immaculate exceptions" doing always those things that please God".**

May God richly bless you in your endeavors; **[Numbers 6: 24-26], "The Lord bless thee and keep thee: The Lord make his face shine upon thee, and be gracious unto thee: The Lord lift up his countenance upon thee, and give thee peace".**

NOTES

NOTES

XI. GREATNESS

What is great or greatness; is it size, is it in quantity? Is it in quality of character as to, for instance, integrity, righteousness, holiness, honorable, that which identifies, and characterizes a person and qualifies them as something above the norm? We have to live with ourselves and whether great or small or anywhere in between; and we do affect others around us influencing and inspiring them to greatness or smallness, depending on our own individual character or lack of it. This affect we have on others, whether good or evil, right or wrong, is what I refer to as **"radiation fallout"**. That which radiates out from your lifestyle falls out, on, and influences others. We do affect our world whether we realize it or not; we all become leaders in some way and to some degree. We can inspire to greatness or degradation; the choice is ours, like it or not, the responsibility is ours.

George Washington was a great leader, general, statesman, and president although he had slaves. I would have to conclude that as a slave owner he treated his slaves well as befitting a person of his stature and character. This is exactly why so many slaves were treated so wretchedly; because their owners were of extremely wretched character. This is why the slave trade came into being to begin with, because of the wretchedness of humanity, and the same reason why it still persists even today around the world in many varieties, especially in the sex trade.

It would be unreasonable to think that the internal qualities that set George Washington apart and identified him as to greatness did not show themselves in his relationship with other people including slaves. He was a Christian, spent considerable time in prayer, owned slaves and as I understand it, even at one time owned a couple of whiskey stills. Maybe he did, maybe he didn't, but in any event he was greatly used of God at a time when this nation in its infancy desperately needed his leadership in war and to establish peace and introduce our nation to greatness. What a tragedy this character of greatness has been lost since George Washington and other statesmen of his day and quality have passed from the scene.

It is said he had horses shot out from under him, bullet holes in his clothes but was never wounded in battle though greatly exposed to the enemy. Certainly God sees things that we do not see, and indeed he does work in mysterious ways his wonders to perform. He certainly has his own ways of getting things done right without governmental interventions, permits, inspections, abiding by a constitution or being concerned about political correctness. It seems like something we need to look into seeing as how the government, our constitution and certainly political correctness are all contaminated by mans input whether God was in it or not. After all God's ways are not our ways for which we can be extremely thankful for his ways are a result of his thoughts, for our ways are a result of our thoughts, **[Isaiah 55: 8-9],** for which our society is paying with much pain and suffering.

A good honest look at the shape our nation is in should be a revelation of our erroneous thinking and mentality. What a tremendous need and challenge for a renewing of our minds. Possibly if we can learn to think more like God thinks maybe, just maybe our ways, our lives, our marriages, our nation will be more conformed to his ways, the ways of righteousness, holiness, with life and life more abundantly and Godly love one for another. It seems like it would be well worth anyone's time and effort as the only things we have to lose is all the misery, heartaches, broken lives, chaos and confusion we have heaped on ourselves by doing things according to our own thoughts and ways.

I would say that it would be a winning situation for man to make an intelligent choice to take God at his word in obedience to his counsel. However, that intelligent part may be a little difficult to grasp. Man hasn't shown himself to have a very good command of that or he wouldn't be in state he is in.

Greatness: would it have any bearing on equality? Where could we find equality between a slave that loves God and serves him and an abusive, mistreating slave owner? No equality there; the slave definitely the more noble of the two regardless of the color; character and stature by far determining the greatness of quality and equality. However if the situation were reversed we would find character and stature still the determining factors with color and position still having nothing to do with it. Nothing, however, justifies slavery in any way or fashion but it is still going on today in many and various forms.

Judah had a few, howbeit very few, good kings that led the people to worship God but many evil kings that caused all the people to sin. Maybe that is where the idea of the separation of church and state originated; just a thought. These kings may have been created equal but they didn't remain that way. They either qualified themselves by intelligent God pleasing choices or disqualified themselves by evil thoughts and ways of iniquity, **[Genesis 6: 5], "And God saw that the wickedness of man was great in the earth and that every imagination of the thoughts of his heart was only evil continually"**. Either way they remained kings until their tenure expired or was terminated, sometimes violently. For those in our post-modern world who scream the loudest about equality, I would have to say, see to your own character, stature and attitudes and see how they measure up to God's will for your life. It just might be you are your own worst enemy.

The majority of us were at one time or another and the vast majority still remains, their own worst enemy, but you don't have to be one of them. God has provided a system of deliverance and his name is Jesus Christ, Saviour and King. If you want equality, rest assured, quality comes first which leads to greatness. No person of true greatness was ever concerned about equality nor demanded it, **[Matthew 18:4; 23:11; Luke 22:26]**. There is a considerable difference between willingly entering into "servant-hood" as opposed to being forced into "servitude". Greatest! It's kind of like humility; once you've determined in your heart you've got it, you've lost it. It's a quality, I'm still working on it that speaks for itself; is silently manifested in an every day lifestyle, not for your benefit but for the benefit of others and above all, the glory of God.

There is much to be learned in this area. Some will never give it a thought, but will stumble through some sort of an existence in servitude by their own ignorance, [lack of knowledge], being deceived, lied to, and lying to themselves, **[Revelation 3:17], and never facing the fact that they are "wretched, and miserable, and poor, and blind, and naked"**. For those of us who have given it considerable thought, we will invest a lifetime perfecting it and still come up short, but still growing in the grace and knowledge of our Lord with his grace being sufficient for us to get us through our failures. When we finally reach the end of our allotted time on this earth, there will still be much left to learn. There is not much doubt but what heaven itself will serve as a glorious learning experience with an eternity in which to learn with wonders to behold beyond our grandest expectations.

NOTES

NOTES

XII. WHAT GOOD HAVE WE DONE

Considering the beginning of our present world as we know it, or the present state and progression of humanity, which had it's beginning in the "Garden of Eden" with Adam and Eve, I can't help but wonder what mankind has accomplished in these past few thousand years. If people cannot bring themselves to believe in heaven or hell as realities: but because we ourselves are obviously realities and what many would consider acceptable proof of our origin, we would at least have to consider both, heaven and hell, with the respective information concerning each, to at least be possibilities.

Now with that established, or at least presented for your consideration, it would certainly follow that there is a probability that we will eventually end up in one of them. It would seem to me, even if these things were just possibilities, that it would be a wise and intelligent thing to prepare for the better of the two, instead of qualifying yourself for the worst of the two by rejecting the qualifications for the best of the two. This would be a very simple and basic choice for anyone with just a maximum of, maybe five to eight percent of their original brain still operative. It is said that is an estimate of how much of it we use from day to day.

Except for a very few that God seems to have granted a special calling, anointing, inspiration, and revelation for specific purposes he had in mind for the furtherance and benefit of humanity, mankind has certainly not shown a propensity for the intelligent use of very much of his brain, that's for sure. Certainly George Washington was one of those special exceptions to whom God also gave special protection during times of warfare to keep him intact to finish what he was called to do. He did have some, it would seem, chosen individuals who were given to assist him in getting America firmly settled on her moorings.

Unfortunately since these individuals went on to their rewards, things have taken a downward turn, especially in the last half century when idiocy seems to have completely torn the moorings loose and set America adrift on the sea of chaos, calamity, and confusion with the rest of the nations of the world wherein we are constantly running afoul of each other. Israel experienced the same thing that we see recorded in [**Judges 2: 7-13**] after the death of their George Washington, Joshua. **"And the people served the Lord all the days of Joshua, and all the days of the elders that outlived Joshua, who had seen all the great works of the Lord,** *that he did for Israel.* **And Joshua the son of Nun, the servant of the Lord, died, being an hundred and ten years old. And they buried him in the border of his inheritance in the mount of Ephraim, on the north side of the hill Gaash.**

Now we get to the crux of the matter that reveals the problems America is having. To continue in verse 10, **And also all that generation were gathered unto their fathers: and there arose another generation after them,** *which knew not the Lord, nor yet the works which he had done for Israel.* Now we find the moorings being torn loose. **And the children of Israel did evil in the sight of the Lord, and served Baalim: And they forsook the Lord God of their fathers, which brought them out of the land of Egypt, and followed other gods, of the gods of the people that were around about them, and bowed themselves unto them, and provoked the Lord to anger. And they forsook the Lord and served Baal and Ashtaroth"**.

Read and study the rest of the accounts of this transgression and rebellion against God and see if you can find any similarity for what America is facing today. Once the good leadership went down the tubes, being replaced by corrupt leadership who knew not the Lord nor what he has done for America or even cared, the people and nation followed soon after. The nations of the world around us are in the condition they are in because of an absence of Godly leadership, and America is rapidly heading in the same direction. Indeed, **"What fools ye mortals be"**! We just cannot seem to learn from the bumps on the other fellows head, and by the time we take our own lumps, it just might be to late. The lumps, the retributions and curses we are suffering today for our sin and abominations are threatening the destruction of America. **[2 Chronicles 7: 14]**: as a blinking light to capture our attention, individually, and collectively, looms before us as the only solution to our dilemmas.

God made it even easier still in **[Deuteronomy 30:19] with a simple choice between life and blessing, death and cursing, and then proceeded to counsel us in the best one to choose with great incentive for such a choice**, *and the vast majority of humanity still insist on making and wallowing in the wrong choices*. And we are supposed to be intelligent beings: that is a difficult one to understand, unless you are familiar with the frailties of man and his additional lack of intelligence in depending on the source that is necessary for the help he needs. First, of course, he is going to have to somehow come up with enough intelligence, a minimum amount would be sufficient, to even realize he is in trouble and needs help. From the evident condition of our world and nation today, it seems that even the minimum amount of intelligence required for such a simple choice is scarce.

We even, though quite young at the time, had to learn how to go potty, feed and clothe ourselves, and unfortunately it seems, there are many who have not advanced very far beyond the first stage. They manage to get dressed, at least partially though yet at times questionably, but their feeding frenzy of junk food, physically, mentally, and spiritually, continues to cast heavy doubt as to their grasp of intelligence. We've all been there; it's just that a few of us decided not to stay there, and fortunately some of us had parents that assisted us in growing out of that situation. [Ephesians 2:1-10] gives a pretty good description of where we were, most still are, before we chose to accept the help God provided for us for our deliverance and salvation. **Thank you Jesus for being that ever present help in time of trouble, [Psalms 46:1].**

But here we are, a couple of millennia later, with great, grand, and noble accomplishments to our credit, or so we think, none of which we could have done if God had not created us in his own image and likeness with the abilities to do such things. Yet man struts around in his pride and arrogance, without any acknowledgment, recognition, or gratitude given to God for designing and enabling man to accomplish such wonderful things. It is so ridiculously simple it is almost comical if it wasn't for the seriousness of the situation. Here we are with all our education, engineers, scientists, experience, technologies, etc. etc. etc. with all the necessary complicated blueprints on how to build, fabricate, and assemble, giant airliners, space vehicles, fly men to the moon and back, huge skyscrapers, huge dams, and the list goes on and on, and yet the vast majority of humanity still have not learned how to follow God's simple plan of salvation to keep their miserable fat out of the fires of eternal hell, and are not even concerned enough to investigate it. With the condition our nation is in, not to mention the rest of the world; the old saying: "Ve get to soon old un to late schmart" has so much truth in it that it's getting quite scary.

To be victimized by others is bad enough, but when we, in our unnecessary, self-imposed stupidity, victimize ourselves, that is intolerable stupidity. Yet here we are, sexual predators on the loose, kidnapping, rape, murdering, and still be allowed it seems, in spite of their already committed atrocities, more freedom and rights than their potential victims. It is well past time for our "leaders" to consider the connection of the porno filth and input that contributes to the influence and arousal of these predators that keeps them going. This too, however, would require an intelligence that seems to be very scarce in this area. The right of one little girl to live, to grow, to develop into the person God created her to be, enjoying his blessings of life and life more abundantly, by far and away trumps all the so called "rights" of the entire porno industry to even exist. If we as a nation, cannot, will not, secure this right for this one little girl, there are many of them: we have, as a nation, in spite of our great accomplishments, failed miserably.

All of our great, grand, glorious, noble, magnanimous accomplishments, and deeds, heaped up in one pile will not buy one soul entrance into God's heaven. **Ye must, Ye must, YE MUST be born again. [2 Peter 1: all], see verse 11, "For so an entrance shall be ministered unto you abundantly into the everlasting kingdom of our Lord and Saviour Jesus Christ".** Study, don't just read, the preceding verses to get a good idea of the requirements for such entrance. Then study to familiarize yourselves with these vs. **4, "great and precious promises and this divine nature".**

Ask yourself, what are these things in **[2 Peter 1: 8-9]** that provide an entrance into God's kingdom, and of what do they consist and then dig for the answers. You'll be amazed at what you will learn if you diligently and with determination apply yourself. There is no end to the revelation information and inspiration that is available to you. You **"gotta get a vision of the value"** of this intimacy with God. It is of greater value than all that is contained in the whole "pile" of human accomplishments and attainments mentioned above. **[Mark 8:36], "For what shall it profit a man to gain the whole world and lose his own soul"**? Jesus did not die for the salvation of the earth, the sun, the moon, the stars; **he died for you, a single solitary soul of greater value than all of the material universe combined. [Isaiah 64:7], "And there is none that calleth upon thy name, that stirreth up himself to take hold of thee".**

Be one of the exceptions to the rule, call upon the name of the Lord, open your Bible for study and meditation, and with diligence and determination, **"stir up yourself to take hold of God".** You have many brethren around you; enlist their support and assistance in your stirring up of yourself to get a hold of God. You'll find you are a blessing to them as well as you search **God's word together and learn together as the Holy Spirit teaches as only he can teach and bring all things to your remembrance, [John 14:26].**

I have to ask the question again, what good have we done? Our prisons are full and we are turning criminals loose to make room for others in our "revolving door policies." The drug culture is rampant, destroying thousands of our young people, the porno industry is alive and "sick", but nevertheless thriving and causing "mentality meltdown" in scores of lives, both young and older, some even graduating into sexual predators whereby we are experiencing kidnappings, rapes, and murders of our young girls, and boys. Hate messages on the internet accessed by the young minds augmented by filth and trash on television have lead to school shootings as well as violence in the homes and on the streets. And our democratic government doesn't even have the intelligence, courage, and decency to encourage the populace to at least investigate this Christian Bible as a possible remedy for all our societal ills and problems.

We are being constantly inundated with this desecration of decency in the land of the free and the home of the brave and we are no longer free to live free because we lack leadership and courage to put an end to the abominations and violence that threatens us all. So to pacify the masses we have much, dialogue, debate, and discussion about the problems with no results as to a solution for solving them. We have extensive spinning of the wheels and slinging of mud, but we can't seem to get out of the ruts of our dilemma's and troubles.

Meanwhile, the instruction manual for the development, operation, and, maintenance of humanity gathers dust on some shelf of rejection and, or neglect in a closet of forgetfulness and locked behind a door of ignorance and locked with a key of stupidity, and the band marches on, **the blind leading the blind completely oblivious to the ditch of destruction just ahead: [Matthew 15:14], "if the blind lead the blind, both shall fall into the ditch".**

There is a very interesting thought in this scenario. Having a blind leader does not require that the ones following must remain blind and continue to follow a blind leader. This world has a super abundance of blind leaders, and certainly a larger number of blind followers, but we do not have to participate. It is good to be free to follow Jesus and choose to think as he has taught and instructed us to think and not be bound unto slavery by the **"sin that doth so easily beset us", [Hebrews 12:1]**, which at one time we all so willingly served, **[Ephesians 2: 1-3]**. **[Philippians 4:7-8] vs. 8, "Finally, brethren, whatsoever things are true, honest, just, pure, lovely, of good report, virtuous, and praiseworthy; think on these things, do them, and the God of peace will be with you". [Galatians 5:22-23] will give you some additional things to think about, "The Fruit of the spirit."**

Do not stop there as some more things to think about await you in your studies that are essential to your spiritual growth and development. The world we live in knows nothing about these things, and couldn't care less about them, unless there is financial gain or pleasure somehow connected with them, but that is to be expected of a Godless society and culture. **[Hebrews 6:9], "But beloved we are persuaded better things of you, and things that accompany salvation, though we thus speak".** The Fruit of the Spirit, **[Galatians 5: 22-23] is a good place to start learning of these "things"** with some additional ones mentioned above to **"think on and do"** to experience the presence of God. We find another example of this Christ-like conduct in **[John 8:29],"And he that sent me is with me: The Father hath not left me alone;** *for I do always those things that please him".* What a glorious example to study and follow.

NOTES

NOTES

XIII. THE GARBAGE COLLECTOR

GARBAGE: by Webster's definition, food waste: REFUSE: trashy writing or speech, my own definition: that which we all would dispose of in a garbage can or otherwise, that is waste that begins to deteriorate, rot, stink, is detestable, to be discarded and disposed of which will contaminate all it comes into contact with if not disposed of quickly and properly. I believe that pretty well covers it; you are welcome to add your own definitions. In reference to Webster's definition of "trashy writing or speech" we can assume with confidence that this must proceed from a living entity, most likely a human being, for instance you or me, or at least someone. The word "trashy" here makes direct reference to the "heart, mind, control center area" we all are in possession of, and the condition of that "heart or mind control center.

We will, for simplicity sake, just refer to it as the heart or the mind as they are basically interchangeable and refer to the same thing, the control center, a God designed, built in computer which we have been given the opportunity to program however our conscience desires with we hope, a bit of common sense thrown in for safety sake. This will preferably be with a sufficient amount of Godly wisdom and intelligence to produce that which is acceptable to God. The use of the words; "trash and refuse" here suggest that this heart, in connection to it's content and abundance of trash and refuse, is a garbage can, or trash can.

There are of course exceptions. **[Matthew 12:34] "O generation of vipers, how can ye, being evil, speak good things? For out of the abundance of the heart the mouth speaketh". [Luke 6:45] "A good man out of the good treasure of his heart bringeth forth that which is good, this is one of the exceptions; and an evil man out of the evil** treasure of his heart bringeth forth that which is evil: for of the abundance of the heart his mouth speaketh". [Titus 1:10] "For there are many unruly and vain talkers and deceivers: especially they of the circumcision". [James 3:8-10] "But the tongue can no man tame; it is an unruly evil, full of deadly poison. Therewith we bless God, even the Father; and therewith curse we men, which are made after the similitude of God. Out of the same mouth proceedeth blessing and cursing. My brethren, these things ought not so to be". [Proverbs 23:7] "For as he thinketh in his heart, so is he". [Genesis 6:5], "And God saw that the wickedness of man was great in the earth and that every imagination of the thoughts of his heart was only evil continually".

There are many other scriptures that make direct reference to, or allude to the heart or mind as to its content and resultant output or "radiation fallout": that which radiates from it and falls out to the good or evil influence of those it touches. [Isaiah 14:12-15] "How art thou fallen from heaven, O Lucifer, son of the morning, which didst weaken the nations! For thou hast SAID IN THINE HEART, I will ascend into heaven, I will exalt my throne above the stars of God: I will sit also upon the mount of the congregation, in the sides of the north: I will ascend above the heights of the clouds; I will be like the most High. Yet thou shalt be brought down to hell, to the sides of the pit". In [Ezekiel 28:11-19] there is more reference to this "Lucifer" more commonly referred to and better understood as the "devil or Satan".

He is referred to in many ways throughout the scriptures that describe him quite well. He is a thief, destroyer, killer, deceiver, liar, false accuser, devourer, etc. etc. Isn't it amazing that multitudes stand in line to be his willing garbage cans, filled with his filth and abominations unto their own destruction, choosing [Deuteronomy 30:19] death and cursing for themselves and their children rather than life and blessing provided by God through [John 3:16] Jesus Christ, Saviour and Lord. Let's take a look at the **15th verse in Ezekiel 28** concerning some interesting points about this "devil", Lucifer. **"Thou wast perfect in thy ways from the day that thou wast created, till INIQUITY was found in thee.** Iniquity, sin, evil, abomination, transgression, rebellion, disobedience, GARGAGE, TRASH: **Spiritual garbage, trash and refuse, polluting the heart and mind, [Romans 7: 24], "O wretched man that I am! Who shall deliver me from the body of this death?** The body of this sinful garbage, trash, filth etc: indeed, who shall deliver us? Who will come and deliver me and collect the garbage with which I have filled my heart, mind, soul and life, my entire being.

Man turns himself into a garbage can **by rejecting and neglecting God's plan of salvation, redemption and reconciliation, being cleansed by the blood Jesus and the "applied" word of God, [John 15:3]. Ephesians 2:1-10] "And you hath he quickened, who were dead [and decomposing] in trespass and sins; Wherein in time past ye walked according to the course of this world, according to the prince of the power of the air, the spirit that now worketh in the children of disobedience:** *Among whom also we all had our conversation in times past in the lusts of our flesh, fulfilling the desires of the flesh and of the MIND; and were by nature the children, garbage cans, of wrath, even as others.*

Verse 4, note: BUT GOD, BUT GOD, BUT GOD, who is rich in mercy, for his great love wherewith he loved us, Even when we were dead [and stinking] in sins, hath quickened us together with Christ, [by grace are ye saved;] And hath raised us up TOGETHER, and made us sit TOGETHER in heavenly places IN Christ Jesus: That in

[and throughout] the ages to come he might show his exceeding riches of his grace in his kindness toward us through Christ Jesus: For by grace are ye saved through faith; and that not of yourselves: it is the gift of God: Not of works lest any man should boast. For we are his workmanship: created in Christ Jesus unto good works, which God hath before ordained that we should walk in them."

We have, as do most people, a garbage can that we throw, cast away, discard, etc, our trash and garbage in for disposal. Occasionally some of it radiates a very foul smell before this process of disposal is complete, and I would well imagine that wherever this refuse goes, it still stinks. Sin is that way, wherever it is, IT STINKS; mans senses are so accustomed to it, they can't smell it, but God is well aware of the condition that thrives, flourishes, and churns within the sinful heart of man. **[Genesis 6:5] "And God saw that the wickedness of man was great in the earth, and that every imagination of his heart was only evil continually".**

I have not as yet had a "garbage collector" have to forcibly take my garbage away from me. I put it in the required pickup place and am quite relieved to see it go. This material garbage, if not disposed of, but allowed to accumulate would become very unpleasant and repulsive, and eventually deadly. It seems to a certain degree, to be comparable to the garbage of sin and iniquity in this respect. There is another comparison were there is an extreme difference between the two. We receive a bill every month from the garbage collection company to get rid of our garbage. It costs to get rid of it, but in the case of sin, it costs to keep it. But like household garbage, it is of great benefit to get rid of your spiritual garbage: it is of eternal benefit as a matter of fact. The "garbage collector" in this case, as with your household garbage, will not force you to give it up. It's your own choice to hand it over willingly; he is ready and anxious to collect it from you, to separate and deliver you from it, but if you want to keep it and wallow in it, he will let you do it. At any rate, the choice is still yours.

It begins with repentance and believing the gospel unto obedience, **[Mark 1: 15]**. Not many people think of God as a "garbage collector" but considering your garbage and its eternal aftermath, if not delivered, you should be very thankful he is your personal "garbage collector", and pickup time is whenever you exercise enough intelligence to get rid of it. What would your home be like if there were no one to clean up the messes we constantly make in the course of living, or the dust and dirt that just seem to accumulate out of nowhere? What if there was no one to collect this lesser garbage together and throw it in the garbage can for the garbage collector to haul away? What if there was no garbage collector to haul it away? I've been in countries were there were none, and trash and garbage were strewn about everywhere; kind of like lives that are lived without regard of the spiritual garbage that is so characteristic of those lives.

It isn't that there is no trash collector for these lives, but they simply will not let him have it. They insist on holding on to it in a self-destruct mode. Jesus is waiting for you to unload on him, **[Matthew 11: 28]**, **"Come unto me, all ye that labour and are heavy laden, and I will give you rest"**. [1Peter 5:7] **"Casting all your care upon him; for he careth for you"**. [I Thessalonians 4:4] gives us some valuable insight concerning this abundance of the heart, **"that every one of you should know how to possess his vessel, his being, in sanctification and honour"**; not allowing it to become a garbage can of iniquity such as in mentioned in the accompanying verses, **verse7, "For God hath not called us, to be garbage cans, unto uncleanness, but to HOLINESS, [Ephesians 3:19],**

"And to know the love of Christ, which passeth knowledge, that ye might be filled with all the fullness of God".

What a wonder it would be to be **"filled with all the fullness of God"** rather than the trash and garbage of the sin of this world that man in his stupidity pursues with such an expenditure of his life and fortune, only to be deposited in the eternal garbage dump of hell. **[1Timothy 6:3-6], verses 5-6, "Perverse disputings of men of corrupt minds, and destitute of the truth,** *garbage cans of iniquity,* **supposing that gain is Godliness: from such withdraw thyself. But Godliness with contentment is great gain".**

This article may offend you, make you angry or whatever, but if it provokes you to consider your own position and where you stand in reference to it and take the necessary steps of correction, then it has done its job and I make no apologies for it. Truth has a way of stirring up and manifesting dirt and trash that has been hidden away under deception much to long. The master garbage collector is waiting to pick up your garbage. Are you going to repent and give it to him or struggle under its weight until it destroys you? **[John 8:31-32; 36], "And Jesus said unto those Jews which believed on him, If ye continue in my word, then are ye my disciples indeed; and ye shall know the truth, and the truth shall make you free. Verse 36, If the Son therefore shall make you free, ye shall be free indeed".**

NOTES

NOTES

XIV. THE PROSPEROUS SOUL

[3 John 1:2], "Beloved, I wish above all things that thou mayest prosper and be in health, even as thy soul prospereth." It would seem that the greatest need of a person is the need of a prosperous soul. Indeed, a prosperous soul is an end that certainly justifies the means to that end, and yet the prosperous soul itself is an evidence that the appropriate means have been employed to an even greater end. A prosperous soul is a soul that is settled in intimacy with God; that has earnestly and effectively executed the means to obtain this position. **[Acts 10:35]** instructs us that it is *the fearing [reverencing] of God and the working of righteousness that is needed to be accepted with God.*

Much has been said and written about *"the fear of the Lord"*. Personally I do not like the use of the word "fear" with its common thought of being frightened, afraid, scared etc, although it does have merit concerning those who reject and oppose God and his truth. However, for the born again believer, I much prefer the word "reverence" for it has a connotation of honor, glory, adoration, worship, and yes, love about it that "fear" does not portray. **[Psalms 111: 10], "The fear of the Lord is the beginning of wisdom: a good understanding have all they that** [study to] ***do* his commandments: his praise endureth forever". [Proverbs 1:7], "The fear of the Lord is the beginning of knowledge: but fools despise wisdom and instruction". [Proverbs 9:10], "The fear of the Lord is the beginning of wisdom: and the knowledge of the holy is understanding".**

At this point in time in an unsaved person's life, a healthy "fear" of the Lord may well be necessary as a prelude to the very beginning of wisdom, knowledge, and understanding. The continuation and development of these will produce reverence to replace the fear that induced the sinner to repent. Now the realization of **[2Timothy 1: 7]** begins to take place: **"For God hath not given us the spirit of fear; but of power, and of love, and of a sound mind." [1 John 4: 18], "There is no fear in love; but perfect love casteth out fear: for fear hath torment. He that feareth is not made perfect in love."** God did not give us a commandment to fear him, **"but to love him with all thine heart, and with all thine soul, and with all thy might" [Deuteronomy 6: 5].**

Also in **[Matthew 22: 37], "**God has commanded us to **"love him with all the heart, soul, mind, strength, indeed the whole being; [Acts 17:28], "In him we live and move and have our being".** This is the relationship of intimacy that God desires to have with us, not one of fear. I realize that one of the meanings of the word "reverence" is fear, but reverence is not a common understanding of fear in our world today. **"There is no fear in love; but perfect love casteth out fear: because fear hath *torment*. He that feareth is not made perfect in love".** Here we see a common use and understanding of "fear". It cannot be connected in any way to the love of God and what is needed for a prosperous soul. But, to honor, love, adore, hold in the highest respect, esteem, awe, and devotion etc; this is to reverence God. This is a foundation on which a soul can obtain prosperity. This is the foundation of Biblical truth that can renew our mind and produce a right spirit and create a clean heart within us.

This is what sets men free and is the basis of God's provision of deliverance, all made available to us through Jesus Christ our Lord and Saviour. To reject such deliverance and its means of employment is to reject life and blessing; instead choosing or remaining in a death and cursing mode and to bring that curse on your own family. **[Deut. 30:19], "Therefore choose life, that both thou and thy seed may live-----".** To reject this means of Gods redemption and then expect to obtain and enjoy it by means of some fictitious religious road that supposedly leads to heaven has got to be the height of stupidity and ignorance and thus man becomes his own worst enemy.

This may seem a bit harsh and offensive to some but I am not interested in trying to be politically correct just to be nice. I would prefer to be Biblically correct even if the truth is offensive to many; **[Romans 3:3-4], "For what if some did not believe? Shall their unbelief make the faith of God without effect? God forbid: yea, let God be true, but every man a liar; as it is written, That thou mightest be justified in thy sayings, and mightest overcome when thou art judged"**. God's truth has always been offensive to the masses and this is no place for diversity. God has given us his word of truth and directions for life. We live by obedience to it, or die by disobedience to it. The choice is ours.

God in his magnificent provision of creating us like he did in his likeness; gave us Godlike abilities and the ability to develop those abilities into God honoring, God pleasing, productive, fruit of righteousness, **[James 3: 18], "And the Fruit of Righteousness is sown in peace of them that make peace"**, producing peaceful lifestyles. For God, **[2 Peter 1:3-4], "According as his divine power hath given us all things that pertain unto life and godliness, through the knowledge of him that hath called us to glory and virtue. Whereby are given to us exceeding great and precious promises: that by these ye might be partakers of the divine nature"**.

This divine nature is Gods own nature, his thinking, his thoughts, and his ways plus any and everything else that is a part of his nature that we can't even begin to comprehend. We fail often in our walk of faith because we neglect to exercise ourselves unto Godliness, **[1 Timothy 4:7]**, but rather have allowed ourselves to get caught up in the **[Mark 4:19]** cares of this world, the deceitfulness of riches, and the lusts of a multitude of other things.

Our nation has become an unruly mob of pleasure seeking, self-serving, wallowing in an "if it feels good, do it mentality". This mad dash for wealth, prosperity, success based on worldly values with whatever else qualifies as the cares of this world, by capturing the attention and affection of man in his lusts of satisfying and pacifying the senses with instant gratification, has sidetracked him from his God intended purpose. He no longer knows nor cares what he was created for or what God desires for him. He is not aware of the fact that each one of us is a part of the whole and he couldn't care less as long as everyone else moves aside and allows him space to exercise "his rights" without interference. What a warped mentality, but that is what the world system has taught him.

Man has one right, and that is to be what God created him to be and do what God created him to do, that which is RIGHT in the eyes of God by his standards, principles, and values and administered by his righteous counsel. What a glorious privilege to be created and chosen by almighty God to partner with him in his vast program of the establishment and administration of his righteousness and holiness; to become an heir and joint heir with Jesus Christ, our Lord and saviour; to everything God owns. It certainly makes all the wealth and riches of this world that so many people sacrifice their lives and eternities to obtain to appear ridiculously insignificant. **Take this whole world but give me Jesus. I won't turn back, I won't turn back.** Do you remember this little chorus we used to sing?

It is amazing how all this temporal, here today and gone tomorrow stuff has, by capturing the affection, crowded out and displaced the soul aware happiness, the fullness of joy and the peace and contentment that comes from and is produced by a life well lived according to the counsel and principles of Jehovah God, creator of life. Unfortunately, even many professing Christians have traded in their **"peace of God [Philippians 4:7], which passeth all understanding and will keep the hearts and minds safe through Christ Jesus."** They have traded this away for the stress and anxieties of this world by neglecting their own personal fellowship with God through the study of his word and the teaching and leading of the Holy Spirit. It seems like we are in a "prodigal son" syndrome, where the pig pen of worldliness has allured and consumed many, not all, but many. Once again, thank God for the exceptions, the **"new creatures in Christ", [2 Corinthians 5:17],** who have given our nation a sense of stability. It is time to come to our senses, arise and be healed in the name of Jesus with our mentalities being healed of the disease of worldliness, **[Romans 12:2]**.

God in his creation of man; manifested and extended to him originally a degree of provision that if acknowledged, and exercised, would have, and will keep man from many of the problems and difficulties he now has to be delivered from. This is because of his idiocy and stupidity in the rejection of the knowledge of who and what he is and how and what he was created to be. God did not create man as a sinful being. We must get this fact settled in the forefront of our thinking. Man is a sinner and sinful because he refuses to accept and embrace Gods provision of redemption and reconciliation he has provided in and through his Son and our saviour Jesus Christ, God's once for all for ever sacrifice for all sin. This burden of sin can be permanently dumped by earnestly **[Mark 1:15], "repenting and believing the gospel of Jesus",** the good news of deliverance. This doesn't mean you won't be tempted from time to time, but it does mean you don't have to be a participant in the temptation, having through Jesus been given dominion over sin.

There still is and always will be all sufficient POWER IN THE BLOOD OF JESUS for man's forgiveness and deliverance from sin. Man must favorably respond to this however, by repentance, turning away from his sinfulness and engaging himself in the learning and establishing of obedience unto God and the **[Acts 10:35] "working of righteousness"**. The reason man is so desperately in need of this secondary help from God is because of his lack of understanding of the primary provision in creating man **[Genesis 1:26] "in his own image, after his own likeness"**. In so doing he designed within man the **[Job 4:21]** God like excellency and wisdom that is held in dormancy by the domination of sin; however God provided a remedy for this situation. **[Luke 15:18], "I will arise and go to my father, and I will say unto him, Father, I have sinned against heaven, and before thee"**.

Repentance, soul depth repentance, will only surface when we finally get sick and tired of existing in the pig pens of this world, realizing the hopelessness of our situation and come to ourselves, arise, swallow our destructive pride and go back to where God always intended us to be, in his house and under his care. It is only here in intimacy with God that this "excellency", this likeness of God, can assume its dominion position and force sin into dormancy and reckoned to be dead. This "excellency" that is in them, the loss and going away of which causes men to die even without wisdom, needs and demands some deep thought and study. Indeed the whole subject of God, his majesty, glory, power, his fullness, warrants and demands much more attention, meditation, and study than even born again Christians give it. This "excellency" has been, for the most part, unacknowledged, and so, undeveloped, and neglected. Consequently, it has neither been pursued nor taught.

Godly excellency must be resurrected and incorporated into each of our lives, becoming the defining characteristic of our Christian culture. If this excellency is missing; we have a very deficient Christian culture and the results are being manifested in our world and indeed many of our churches today. I am appalled at the permissiveness in the area of sex perversion that is not only permitted but encouraged by its being allowed and embraced for the sake of "tolerance" in some churches today with the constant debate and dialogue that is engaged in about it. What part of God's saying "no" don't these people understand? It is amazing how man continues to attempt end runs around God in their feeble attempts to get His blessings without meeting the requirements He has set down.

Neither is man concerned about God's counsel on this and other situations and matters of transgressions. You would think that we actually had a voice in the matter when God himself has already passed judgment on such filth and abominations. Doesn't "thus saith the Lord" have any meaning in these religious institutions anymore, or the lives of those who attend such organizations? These are those that **[Matthew 15: 8; Mark 7: 6], draweth nigh unto God with there mouth, and honoureth with their lips, but their heart is far from Him"**. We see the **"Woes"** of **[Isaiah 5]** presenting themselves in these situations.

How can the excellency of Godliness prevail against such opposition when there is more concern about maintaining political correctness, diversity, and tolerance of adversity in evil indulgence than there is about standing your ground for Biblical truth and correctness? Where are the voices of our spiritual leaders, our "mighty men" in regard to these matters? They come on television talk shows for debate when there is no room for debate, the matter already being settled. God has already settled these matters in his word. There is no place for tolerance, diversity, acceptance or any other excuse for inclusion in these matters. Neither are the "civil rulers, the judges etc." of our nation exempt from blame in these matters even though they attempt to hide behind this so called "constitutional separation of church and state". It isn't even in the constitution and has been deviously used primarily as a means of separation of God and people and as an excuse for our civil leaders not to be involved in the support and encouragement of the Christian religion as the foundation on which America was built.

They could and should do this as a duty and responsibility to the nation and its people and it can be done without establishing it as a state church. It, of course, should never be pushed aside to make room for other cultures, concepts, and religions to take root that never contributed anything of a positive nature toward the acknowledging of almighty God and his providence in his establishing of this great nation. I understand that the embracing of other religions may be politically correct but once again I must stress the importance of being Biblically correct. Politically correctness is an **"evil invention of man"**, **[Romans 1: 30]**, and as such is immensely inferior to Biblical correctness for God has commanded**, thou shalt worship the Lord thy God, and him only shalt thou serve.** Other religions worship and serve other gods and thus disqualify themselves as worthy to stand with the Christian religion. We do not make this judgment; God himself has already made it. It is up to us to agree with him and be obedient and faithful without compromise.

Having shown weakness in compromising, now it is demanded and expected as a "Christian obligation" to show compassion, kindness, understanding, and of course, tolerance and diversity. If you don't mind my saying so: as a matter of fact, if you do mind my saying so; what a bunch of garbage! We don't seem to have learned yet that **"a little leaven leaveneth the whole lump"**, **[1 Corinthians 5: 6; Galatians 5: 6]**. It would seem, from general observation, that the compromising has in many cases cost us the battle. And still, even after taking the lumps on our own heads, we haven't learned our lessons very well. Let's hope the future holds better results than our past has afforded us. But that is still "our choice".

God is a much better transmitter of his word than we are receivers, a much better teacher than we are as students. He has a full understanding and knowledge of everything, both of the things on earth and of things above, whereas our understanding and knowledge is somewhat fragmented and in many cases wholly inadequate concerning the things above as well as things of this world. We have been instructed to **[Colossians 3:2], "Set your affection on the things above, not on things on the earth".** We can get some insight here into the direction God is trying to take us as to its overall importance. We get ourselves trapped into the things that restrict us to an **existence** and pursue them while God is trying to elevate our minds, thus our lives, to things above such as wisdom, knowledge, and understanding. There is also this other overlooked, neglected, undeveloped, and seldom used item that needs considerable attention; "intelligence". *Intelligence and wisdom are much the same, however even with great knowledge, intelligence is needed to know how it should be applied, wisdom when to apply it, and understanding as to why it should be applied.*

These things may well interchange and overlap in their application and use, but all are absolutely necessary, and if properly applied will provide the things of earth that are needed to sustain and provide for life here today. Wisdom, however governs it all and its application is essential not only to the things of life here on earth, but also to the securing of life and life more abundantly here and in the life to come. Wisdom is both developed and asked for, however it is much easier developed if it is first asked for. **[James 1:5], "If any of you lack wisdom, let him ask of God, that giveth to all men** liberally, and upbraideth not; and it shall be given him"**. The manner or manners by which God dispenses this thing known as wisdom is a subject to be studied and learned, being attained to by much study and learning, **[Proverbs 1: 7], "The fear of the Lord is the beginning of knowledge: but fools despise wisdom and instruction"**, including the instruction that results in wisdom.

There is the wisdom of this world; that which man scrapes together out of his own reasoning without consideration of God. This is that which **"is foolishness with God," [1 Corinthians 3:19]**. It is mans reliance on his own conjured up attempt at wisdom, without regarding of God and his wisdom. Self reliance without God is what has brought man to his degraded state of being, but then, once again **[Proverbs 1:7], "The fear of the Lord is the beginning of knowledge but fools despise wisdom and instruction"**. It is amazing how often pertinent scriptures fit perfectly into so many situations and categories. Some would call this redundancy; I call it application and emphasis for learning and effect. Wisdom and instruction provide understanding and knowledge and Biblical intelligence will pursue them all.

Is God so small that his fullness can be comprehended and contained in our present level of thinking and thought, or, is there a place for exploration into the area of **[Isaiah 55: 8-9]**? These vastly unexplored regions of Gods thoughts and ways will provide the most rewarding and exciting discoveries that are beyond mans imaginations. **[1Corinthians 2:9], "But as it is written, Eye hath not seen, nor ear heard, neither hath entered into the heart of man, the things, which God hath prepared for them that love him"**. Verse 10 continues; **But God hath revealed them to us by his Spirit: for the Spirit searcheth all things, yea the deep things of God"**. Interesting things are in store for those who will set themselves to explore the wonders of God and refuse to be limited by the confines, wisdom, intimidations, and accusations of this world. God has freely given us the invitation, opportunities and privilege of exploration and attaining to the glories and wonders he has set before us. We must renew our minds, upgrade and enlighten our mentalities by way of Gods counsel, directions, and provisions to enter into this greatest of all relatively unexplored, unrealized frontiers of his greatness. It is time to, **Arise and be Healed in the name of Jesus** of our lethargy, laziness, ignorance and stupidity.

These are all conditions of our own making. America has no one to blame but ourselves for such foolishness. But this is the same with any nation or people. We entangle ourselves in webs of our own weaving and invariably find someone else to blame for the resulting problems of entanglement. There are exceptions, of course when we find ourselves in a warfare of some sort, created by someone else's stupidity, for a change, maybe not our own:, however, **[James 4: 1-10], "From whence come wars and fightings among you? Come they not hence, even of your lusts that war in your members"**. I invite you to read and study all 10 verses to see if any of them apply in your individual lifestyle. Being human, there is no doubt, you will find some. Have a good and productive study and may God bless you richly.

NOTES

www.ingramcontent.com/pod-product-compliance
Lightning Source LLC
LaVergne TN
LVHW021711060526
838200LV00050B/2613